AF653899

CHAKMA ISSUE IN THE POLITICS OF ARUNACHAL PRADESH

About the Author

Gautam Chakma teaches Political Science in Tripura Central University. He obtained his PhD degree in Political Science from North Eastern Hill University (NEHU), Shillong. He did a Certificate Programme in Development, Law and Social Justice offered by the International Institute of Social Studies (ISS), The Hague, The Netherlands. His research areas include, inter alia, Migration Studies, Politics in North East India and Political Theory. He has guided several PhD scholars concerning problems of North East India and international relations

Chakma Issue in the Politics of Arunachal Pradesh

GAUTAM CHAKMA

Akansha Publishing House
Delhi • Guwahati • Visakhapatnam

AKANSHA PUBLISHING HOUSE
4649/21-B, Ansari Road
Daryaganj, New Delhi - 110 002
Phones: 23263193, 9435116718
Email: ektabooks@yahoo.com
Visit us: www.akanshapublishinghouse.com

Chakma Issue in the Politics of Arunachal Pradesh

© Author

First Published, 2022

ISBN 978-81-8370-632-2

[All rights reserved. No part of this publication may be reproduced, stored in retrieval system or transmitted, in any form or by any means, mechanical, photocopying, recording or otherwise, without the prior written permission of the author/publisher. Views expressed in the papers published in the book are those of the contributors and the editor(s), publisher do not hold any responsibility.]

PRINTED IN INDIA

Published by Akansha Publishing House, New Delhi - 110 002

This book is
Dedicated to
the CHAKMAS
and all other people
of Arunachal Pradesh

Preface

This book is a compilation of chapters that discuss the processes of ethnic and party politics in Arunachal Pradesh *vis-à-vis* the Chakma citizenship issue. Having discussed the background of migration and resettlement of the Chakmas in the state, the book examines the manner in which various socio-political organizations of the state responded to the issue such as the responses of All Arunachal Pradesh Students Union (AAPSU), the responses of various political parties like the INC, and the Peoples' Party of Arunachal (PPA). Chapter IV examines the Centre-State conflict in relation to the Chakma issue while Chapter V examines ethno-politics of Arunachal Pradesh in response to the issue. Chapter VI provided the major conclusions followed by observations. In the book, constant effort has been made to understand the difficult concepts of the subject as easy and informative as possible for the readers.

Being a Chakma himself, the author has tried his best to be as neutral as possible with the analysis of facts and data collected from various sources. As far as the concluding chapter is concerned, certain criticism might come from some corners. The only defence is that he has done what he should have done as a researcher. It is hoped that the book will be an immense source of academic research.

Contents

Abbreviations

AAPSU	All Arunachal Pradesh Students' Union
AASU	All Assam Students' Union
AAGSP	All Assam Gana Sangram Parishad
AC	Arunachal Congress
AICCC	All India Chakma Cultural Conference
AI	Amnesty International
APCYF	Arunachal Pradesh Chakma Youths' Federation
APCGA	Arunachal Pradesh Chakma Gaonburah Association
APP	Arunachal Pradesh Police
APHSU	Arunachal Pradesh Hajong Students Union
APC	Arunachal People's Conference
AGP	Asom Gana Parishad
AWJF	Arunachal Women's Justice Forum
BJP	Bharatya Janata Party
CCRCAP	Committee for Citizenship Rights of the Chakmas of Arunachal Pradesh
CHT	Chittagong Hill Tracts
CNCI	Chakma National Council of India
CNCIAP	Chakma National Council of India Arunachal Pradesh
CRDO	Chakma Rights and Development Organisation

CWWS	Chakma Women Welfare Society
DCSU	Delhi Chakma Students' Union
INC	Indian National Congress
IWGIA	International Work Group for Indigenous Affairs
JAC	Joint-Action-Committee
JD	Janata Dal
JP	Janata Party
MLA	Member of Legislative Assembly
NHRC	National Human Rights Commission of India
NDA	National Democratic Alliance
NEFA	North East Frontier Agency
NEITPF	North East Indigenous Tribal Peoples' Forum
NGO	Non-Governmental Organization
NSCN-IM	National Socialist Council of Nagaland of Isak and Muivah
OAU	Organization of African Unity
OCCHTC	Organizing Committee Chittagong Hill Tracts Campaign
PIL	Public Interest Litigation
PPA	Peoples' Party of Arunachal
PRO	Peoples' Rights Organization
SCI	Supreme Court of India
SI	Survival International
UNHCR	United Nations High Commissioner for Refugees
USAID	United States Agency for International Development

List of Tables

CHAPTER - I

Introduction: Migration and Resettlement of the Chakmas in Arunachal Pradesh

The demand made in an Appeal by the Peoples' Referendum Rally of Arunachal Pradesh on September 20, 1995, stating that "*The refugee problem is a burning issue in our peaceful State of Arunachal Pradesh. Their demand for permanent citizenship rights is creating panic among the bona fide people. Considering the serious nature of the problem .... We demand Chakma refugees to quit Arunachal Pradesh,*"[1] shows the genesis of the Chakma issue in the politics of Arunachal Pradesh concerning which this study has been pursued. The present Chakma issue in the politics of Arunachal Pradesh has emanated from the background of migration and resettlement of Chakma refugees in the State way back in 1964. Refugee resettlement has had wide ranging ramifications for societies and polities of the recipient

1 Organizing Committee Peoples' Referendum Rally, *An Appeal*, Naharlagun, Arunachal Pradesh, September 20, 1995.

countries. It is not just the shifting and resettlement of people from one place of abode to another but also most fundamental to the understanding of the ever changing 'space content' and 'space relations' of an area.[2] Refugee resettlement is found to have affected both the demographic and economic balance of groups within a given space. Hence, the protection of space and economic opportunities has become central objectives of the local population, while expansion of opportunities within that space has become the central objectives of migrant population.[3]

Resettlement of refugees has also changed the political structures and the mode of politics of a given area. The size, composition and distribution of population in relation to both government and politics have undergone a change as a result of refugee resettlement.[4] In multiethnic societies, refugee resettlement has led to intense conflicts between the refugee settlers and the local population. Politics over the fear of land alienation, perceived demographic and political threats, xenophobia, and identity crisis have become prominent in places affected by refugee migration.[5] In most cases, the question of citizenship rights of the refugees has become the single most important source of ethnic-conflict and power politics of 'who gets what, from whom and how

2 For details see, V. C. Sinha and E. Zacharia, *Elements of Demography,* (New Delhi: Allied Publishers, 1984), pp. 95-115.

3 Myron Weiner, *Sons of the Soil: Migration and Ethnic Conflict in India*, (Delhi: Oxford University Press, 1978), pp. 3-4.

4 Myron Weiner and Michael S. Teitelbaum, *Political Demography, Democratic Engineering,* (New York: Berghahn Books, 2001), p. ix.

5 Nicholas Van Hear, *New Diasporas: The Mass Exodus, Dispersal and Regrouping of Migrant Communities*, (London: UCL Press, 1998), p. 1.

much.'[6] In such a situation, ethnic loyalty has been mobilized and manipulated by political parties and other social groups as in the case of Chakma citizenship issue in the politics of Arunachal Pradesh.

Ethnic politics has usually been referred to the art of ethnic political mobilization often in a relational framework between the native ethnic groups and the outsiders such as refugees. Ethnic politics is shaped by constraints imposed by outsiders. Thus, the internal 'we' (*ethnos* in Greek) has been distinguished from the external 'aliens' (*ethnikos* in Greek). Where no relevant outsiders exist, the necessity for ethnic politics disappears. The need of ethnic politics arises only when strange, threatening, competitive outsiders must be confronted.[7] Ethnicity as politics is meaningful only in such a relational framework. Further, in ethnic politics, outsiders are viewed negatively as threats to generate political interests and internal coherence. Ethnic politics is cultural mobilization of the *ethnos* or 'we' in relation to *ethnikos* or 'others.'[8] On the other hand, ethnic politics also refers to politics of assertion on the part of 'others' protesting the domination of the native elites.

Chakma refugees resettled in Arunachal Pradesh surfaced as a burning issue as 'outsiders' vs.'natives' only in 1992 when the Central government announced to grant citizenship to the Chakmas. The problem has then become the central agenda of debate not only in the Parliament but also in the Assembly of Arunachal

---

6 Urmila Phadnis, "Ethnic Groups in the Politics of Sri Lanka," in David Taylor and Malcolm Yapp (eds.), *Political Identity in South Asia*, (London: Curzon Press, 1979), p. 192.

7 Milton Jecob Esman, *Ethnic Politics*, (New York: Cornell University Press, 1994), p. 1.

8 For details see, Iris Marion Young, *Justice and Politics of Difference*, (Princeton NJ: Princeton University Press, 1990), pp. 2-10.

Pradesh and the National Human Rights Commission. The whole issue centers on the question of citizenship of the Chakmas in Arunachal Pradesh. The issue became complex as it relates not only to the citizenship question of the Chakmas who actually migrated but also the Chakmas who are born within the state of Arunachal Pradesh during last half a century.

According to the 2011 Census of India, Arunachal Pradesh is said to be the least refugee affected state in India even after considering the presence of Chakma (40,000), Hajong (5,000) and Tibetan (10,000) refugees. Whereas the neighboring state of Assam hosts 12 million refugees. The total population of Assam's capital city of Guwahati itself is double the total population of Arunachal Pradesh. Arunachal Pradesh is also the most thinly populated state in the country with a population density of 17 persons per square kilometer (2011 Census of India).[9] The demand to remove the Chakmas from Arunachal Pradesh came after three decades of their settlement in the state. The citizenship issue of the Chakmas has been politicized by the socio-political organizations of Arunachal Pradesh for mass mobilization and power politics rather than to find a solution. This has been evident from the way different social organizations of the state such as the All Arunachal Pradesh Students' Union (AAPSU), political parties, and the State and Central Governments have responded to the issue. However, a discussion on migration, displacement and refugee resettlement will help better understand the Chakma issue in the politics of Arunachal Pradesh.

Meaning and Definition of Migration

The word 'migrate' has been derived from Latin word *migrare,* which means to move from one place or country

9 For details see, Census of India: Provisional Population Tables - Census 2011, *censusindia.gov.in.* pp. 3-10.

to another for permanent or semi-permanent settlement.[10] People who migrate are called "migrants," or "settlers," depending on historical setting, circumstances and perspective. Migration that occurs for economic reasons is called 'voluntary' migration. In most cases, migration involves force that push people out of a place or country.[11] Such migration of people has been defined as 'involuntary' or 'forced migration' (also called deracination – originally a French word meaning uprooting). It often connotes violent coercion, and is used interchangeably with the concepts of 'displacement' or forced displacement.[12] Thus, those who have experienced forced migration are termed as "forced migrants", "displaced persons", or "refugees" although the term 'refugee' has restricted legal connotation.

The term refugee has been derived from the Latin word called *refugium* meaning "shelter, security, a haven."[13] The classical institutional definition of refugee is found in the 1951 United Nations Convention on

---

10 William Petersen, "A General Typology of Migration," in Robin Cohen (ed.), *Theories of Migration,* (Cheltenham: Edward Elgar Publishing Ltd., 1996), p. 4.

11 Everett S. Lee, "A Theory of Migration," in Robin Cohen (ed.), *Theories of Migration*, (Cheltenham: Edward Elgar Publishing Ltd., 1996), p. 16.

12 For details see, A. Speare Jr., "The Relevance of Models of Internal Migration for the Study of International Migration", in G. Tapinos (ed.) *International Migration Proceedings of a Seminar on Demographic Research in Relation to International Migration,* (Paris: Committee for International Cooperation in National Research in Democracy (CICRED), March 5-11, 1974), pp. 84-94.

13 For details see, Anthony J. Bevilacqua, "Who is a Refugee? Distinction between Economic and Political Determinants of Refugee Movements," in Joseph M. Kitagawa (ed.), *American Refugee Policy: Ethical and Religious Reflections*, (New York: Fund for World Relief, 1983), p. 37.

Refugees. The 1951 United Nations Convention Relating to the Status of Refugees later extended by the 1967 Protocol, defined refugees as:

> Any person who, owing to well-founded fear of being persecuted for reasons of race, religion, nationality, membership of a particular social group or political opinion, is outside the country of his nationality and is unable or, owing to such fear, is unwilling to avail himself of the protection of that country; or who, not having nationality and being outside the country of his former habitual residence, is unable or, owing to such fear, is unwilling to return to it.[14]

According to the United Nations High Commissioner for Refugees (UNHCR), there are now 22 million refugees around world who have been forced to leave their countries to escape from political persecution, armed conflict or violence and forced displacement.[15]

A broader meaning of 'refugee' has been provided by the Organization of African Unity (OAU, 1969) which defined refugees as:

Every person who, owing to external aggression, occupation, foreign domination, or events seriously disturbing public order in either part or whole of his country of origin or nationality, is compelled to leave his place of habitual residence in order to seek refuge in another place outside his country of origin or nationality.[16]

---

14 Article 1, 1951 UN Convention Relating to the Status of Refugees, on *Refworld* CD-Rom, UNHCR, 1997.

15 UNHCR, *The State of the World's Refugees, 1997-98: A Humanitarian Agenda,* (New York: Oxford University Press Inc., 1997), p. 2.

16 Article 1, 1969 OAU Convention Governing the Specific Aspects of Refugee Problems in Africa, on *Refworld* CD-Rom, UNHCR, 1997.

Table 1.1 A General Typology of Migration

Relation	Migratory force	Class of Migration	Type of Migration	
			Conservative	Innovating
Nature and man	Ecological Push	Primitive	Wandering	Flight from the land
			Ranging	
State (or equivalent)and man	Migration Policy	Forced	Displacement	Slave Trade
		Impelled	Flight	Cooli Trade
Man and his norms	Higher aspiration	Free	Group	Pioneer
Collective behavior	Social momentum	Mass		

Source: William Petersen, "A General Typology of Migration," in Robin Cohen (ed.), *Theories of Migration,* (Cheltenham: Edward Elgar Publishing Ltd., 1996), p. 4.

The concept of forced migration is important because it is associated with persecution, war and displacement and also it has become a topic of serious study and discussion in the recent past. This increased attention is the result of the creation of an international legal structure of human rights, Court actions and the realizations that forced migration has created destabilizing effects for societies and polities especially in parts of Africa and Asia such as India and Pakistan.

Another subset of forced migration is development-induced displacement. Such displacement forced communities and individuals out of their homes, often also their homeland. Such displacement is historically associated with the construction of hydroelectric dams as that of the Kaptai dam that displaced the Chakmas of Arunachal Pradesh in 1964.[17] Hence, the present study has been accommodated in the ambit of forced migration defined by the International Organization of Migration as any person who migrates to "escape persecution, conflict, repression, and man-made disasters like dam, ecological degradation, or other situations that endanger lives, freedom or livelihood"[18] for conceptual understanding.

Types of Migration

Migration is a differential phenomenon with distinguishable character. There is a growing diversity in migration particularly in relation to its cause, distance, duration, selectivity and motivation. The relatively permanent movement of people from one place to another

17 For details see, Anti Slavery Society, *Chittagong Hill Tracts: Militarization, Oppression and the Hill Tribes,* (London: Anti Slavery Society, 1984), pp. 15-25.

18 For details see, Alexander Betts, *Forced Migration and Global Politics,* (Oxford: Wiley-Blackwell, 2009), pp.1-20.

within a country is referred to as *in-migration* and *out-migration,* but when the movement is between countries it is referred as *immigration* and *emigration*. The place of in-migration or immigration is called the *receiver population,* and the place of out-migration or emigration is called the *sender population*. There are two basic types of migration studied by demographers: *internal migration* and *international migration*.

Migration literature also speaks of a third classification: *forced migration*. Forced migration exists when a person is moved against his or her will, for example, a slave, or when the move is initiated because of external factors (persecution or civil war).

The distinction between internal and international migration is crucial because they happen for different reasons. Structural barriers are more likely to impede the mobility of a potential international migrant than an internal migrant. This is because international migration involves more administrative procedures, greater expense, longer distance and more difficulties associated with obtaining employment, accessing state services, and learning a new language. The motivations behind international migration are usually stronger than those behind internal migration. International migration carries greater political and demographic significance than that of the internal migration as it brings about either gain or loss to a country's population. Table 1.1 shows a general typology of human migration provided by William Petersen.

Internal Migration

This refers to a change of residence within national boundaries, for example, between states, provinces, cities, or municipalities. Internal migration occurs owing to several socio-economic factors. Internal migration can be classified as (a) rural to urban, (b) urban to urban or intra-urban, (c) rural to rural or intra-rural, and (d) urban to rural.

Migration from a *rural* to an *urban* area becomes obvious when facilities and opportunities of human life are abundant in the latter. In the urban areas there are better facilities and opportunities in the fields of education, employment, health services, sports, and income generation. Rural-urban migration is primarily a response to economic motives. In effect, the rural to urban migration transforms society rural to urban.[19]

The movement of people from one urban area to another is termed as or *intra-urban* migration.[20] This kind of migration takes place because larger cities provide relatively better facilities, work-wages and opportunities than in the smaller cities. As a result, big cities are growing unevenly.

In non-industrialized-agrarian economies, large migration occurs from rural to rural area which is described as *intra-rural* mobility. This type of migration originates from the areas with lower per capita productivity and incomes to areas with a higher per capita agricultural productivity and incomes.

The excessive urbanization and uneven development in large cities, particularly in the wake of the Second World War generated a counter migration from urban to rural areas. Over population in the cities and depopulation in rural areas are said to be the reasons behind such type of migration as evident in most European countries, the United States of America and even in some developing

---

19 W. A. V. Clark, *Human Migration*, (New Delhi: Sage Publications, 1986), p. 25.

20 *Ibid.*, p. 12.

countries. These are some of the major internal migration variety generated by the push and pull factors having both negative and positive effects.

International Migration

International migration refers to change of residence across national boundaries. An international migrant is someone who moves to a different country. International migrants may be classified as legal immigrants, illegal immigrants, and refugees. Legal immigrants are those who moved with the legal permission of the receiver nation. Illegal immigrants are those who moved without legal permission, and refugees are those crossed an international boundary to escape persecution and displacement.

Large-scale international migrations occurred mainly between 1800 and 1939 from Europe to other regions of the world. In fact, with the emergence of large number of nation-states after the Second World War, the problem of international migration has rather proliferated.[21]

The European immigrations, particularly the Portuguese and the Spanish to Latin America are considered as relatively modern and important international migration. Among other emigrants who made migrations to North America were the British, French, German and the Irish. The majority of the immigrants from the European continent moved to the United States, which is said to have hosted over 35 million people of British origin between 1850 and 1914.[22] Similarly, North and South America, Australia, New Zealand, South Africa, Zimbabwe, Kenya and Canada

---

21 Stephen Castles and Mark J. Miller, *The Age of Migration: International Population Movements in the Modern World,* (Basingstoke: Palgrave, 2003), p. 4.

22 Gérard Chaliand and Jean-Pierre Rageau, *The Penguin Atlas of Diasporas,* (New York: Viking, 1995), p. xviii.

were major destinations for European emigrants, particularly the British.

These large migration flows influenced the process of nation state formation in many ways. The diaspora cultures and myths reflected the importance of migration to the foundation of certain nations, like the American "melting pot" nation.[23] The transnational labor migration fell to a lower level from 1930s to the 1960s and then rebounded.[24]

Since the second half of the twentieth century, some major international migrations have also occurred from countries within less developed European periphery and parts of the Third World into northern Europe during the 1960s; from Latin America to the USA throughout the period after 1965; from Asia to America, Australia, New Zealand, and even more within Asia itself, during the 1960s and 1980s; and from the former socialist political systems of Eastern Europe and old Soviet Union after 1989. This movement of people across the globe has become an important component of understanding the "globalization" of world economy.[25]

Theories of Migration

Theories of migration are important because they can help us explain and understand the causes and effects of any particular migration phenomenon in its wider social and political contexts. Because of the fact that people migrate for various reasons, migration has

---

23 Nathan Glazer *et al*, *Beyond the Melting Pot*, (Massachusetts: The M. I. T. Press, 1970), p. 288.

24 For details see, Patrick Manning, *Migration in World History*, (New York: Routledge, 2005), pp. 145-50.

25 Nicholas Abercrombie *et al*, *The Penguin Dictionary of Sociology*, (London: Penguin Books Ltd., 2000), p. 227.

acquired different theories advanced by diverse scholars ranging from political scientists, sociologists, demographers and geographers to economists, historians and lawyers. Four major theories of migration – Rational Choice Theory, Migration Systems Theory, World Systems Theory, and Transition Theory have been discussed here.

Rational Choice Theory of Migration

The earliest rational choice explanations of forced migration can be traced in two of E. G. Ravenstein's celebrated papers under the title "The Laws of Migration" published in the *Journal of the Royal Statistical Society* of England in 1885 and 1889 respectively.[26]

According to Ravenstein, every act of migration involves a driving force. He has drawn this conclusion from his observation on migration flows across Europe and North America during the second half of the nineteenth century as a result of the "disruptive influence of Industrial Revolution." Industrial Revolution displaced millions of people from their traditional homes and livelihoods leading to their migration all across frontiers in search of a better life or to escape one that had become intolerable.

At the heart of Ravenstein's emerging migration model are the concepts of *absorption* and *dispersion*. He defines a country of absorption as having "a population more or less in excess of the number of its natives." As migrants move toward absorption centers, they leave

26 For details see, E. G. Ravenstein, 'The Laws of Migration,' *Journal of the Royal Statistical Society,* Vol. 48, No. 2, (London: The Royal Statistical Society, June, 1885), pp. 167-235; E. G. Ravenstein, 'The Laws of Migration,' *Journal of the Royal Statistical Society,* Vol. 52, No. 2, (London: The Royal Statistical Society, June, 1889), pp. 241-305.

"gaps" that are filled up by migrants from more remote districts, creating migration flows that reach out to "the most remote corner of the kingdom."

From Ravenstein's point of view migration is "change and progress in human life from sedentary stagnation."[27] People migrate from one country to another basically for economic compulsions. But what is important for Ravenstein is that such movement of people is not likely to take place lawless. His emphasis is that migration is guided by certain laws or rules which he is said to have derived from his analysis of nineteenth-century population data for England. Ravenstein's laws of migration can be stated as follows:[28]

1. People are more willing to travel long distances to occupy unsettled land than they would in a country more fully settled.
2. Most migrants are adults.
3. Migration motivated people proceeds step by step.
4. Migrants going long distances generally go by preference to one of the great centers of commerce or industry.
5. The residents of towns are less migratory than those of rural areas.
6. Large cities grow more by migration than by natural increase.
7. Each current of migration produces a compensating counter current.
8. Migration differentials (such as gender, social class, age) influence a person's mobility.
9. The major causes of migration are economic.

---

27 Ronald Skeldon, *Migration and Development: A Global Perspective,* (London: Addison Wesley Longman Ltd., 1997), p. 19.

28 *Ibid.,* p. 19.

The seminal significance of Ravenstein's theory of migration lies in the fact that several of his generalizations are still worth testing and helpful not only to explain why people migrate for economic reasons within a country but also to explain why people move from one country to another for various other reasons such as "persecution" that caused the Chakma migration to Arunachal Pradesh.

Push and Pull Theory of Migration

Rational choice explanation of migration can also be had from push and pull theory. Although push and pull theory of migration is a reformulated version of Ravenstein's theory, it gives us more systematic guidelines as to why people move. Its chief exponent, Everett S. Lee, postulates that migration from one place to another occurs in a "push-pull" formation; that is, unfavorable conditions in one place "push" people out, and favorable conditions in an external location "pull" them out. This "push" and "pull" gravity works like antinomies or, in a more sophisticated version, through "asymmetrical dyads," with one pole more strongly affirmed than the other.[29]

The push and pull theory defines migration as permanent or semi-permanent change of residence involving an origin, a destination and an intervening set of obstacles.[30] The factors which enter into the decision to migrate and the process of migration have been summarized by Everett S. Lee in the following four headings:

1. Factors associated with the area of origin.
2. Factors associated with the area of destination.

---

29 Robin Cohen, (ed.), *Theories of Migration*, (Cheltenham and Brookfield: Edward Elger Publishing Company, 1996), p. xi.

30 For details see, Everett S. Lee, n. 11, pp. 14-24.

3. Intervening obstacles.
4. Personal factors.

In every country there are countless factors which push people out, for example, 'persecution' as minus factor may push people out to a proximate country. The safety situation in the country of refuge may be described as plus factor. However, migration for any reason, economic or political, whether within or outside the country and however stronger the push-pull gravity may be, does not take place 'obstacle' free. In fact, structural barriers like long distance and rugged passage, old and minor family members, rules of entry in case of international migration, difficulties associated with earning of livelihood at destination, and learning a new language in a new place impede peoples' mobility.[31] Table 1.2 shows + and – signs inside the circles and intervening obstacles in between the circles.

Table 1.2 Plus (+) and Minus (–) Factors at Origin and Destination

Origin and destination factors and intervening obstacles in migration

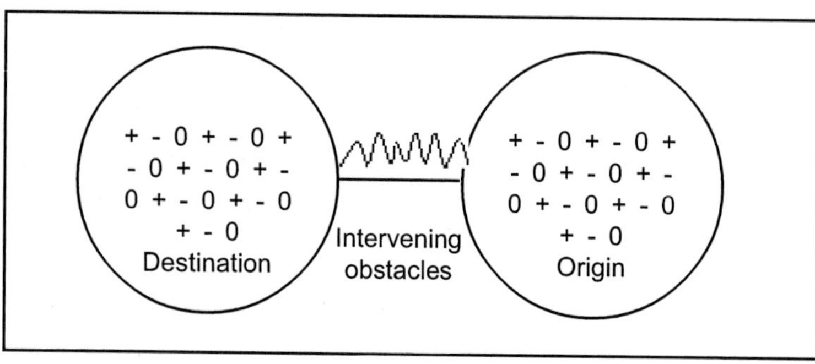

Source: Everett S. Lee, "A Theory of Migration," in Robin Cohen (ed.), *Theories of Migration,* (Cheltenham: Edward Elgar Publishing Ltd., 1996), p. 17.

31 For details see, Everett S. Lee, n. 11, p. 16.

On the basis of plus (+) and minus (–) factors analysis, Lee has drawn a series of hypotheses about the volume of migration under varying conditions, the development of stream and counter-stream, and the characteristics of migrants.

Volume of Migration

1. The volume of migration within a given territory varies with the degree of diversity of areas included in that territory.
2. The volume of migration is related to the difficulty of surmounting the intervening obstacles.
3. Unless severe checks are imposed, both volume and rate of migration tend to increase with time.

Stream and Counter-stream:

1. Migration tends to take place largely within well defined streams.
2. For every major migration stream, a counter-stream develops.
3. The efficiency of stream and counter-stream tends to be low if origin and destination are similar.

Characteristics of Migrants:

1. Migration is selective.
2. Migrants responding primarily to plus factors at destination tend to be positively selected.
3. Migrants responding primarily to minus factors at origin tend to be negatively selected; or where the minus factors are overwhelming to entire population groups, they may not be selected at all.

4. The characteristics of migrants tend to be intermediate between the characteristics of the population at origin and the population at destination.

Systems Theory of Migration

Systems explanation of migration was first offered by Akin L. Mabogunje. This approach is designed to answer questions such as: why and how does a person become a refugee or an immigrant? What changes does he undergo in process? What effects have these changes both on the place from where he comes and on the place to which he moves? Are there situations or institutions which force people to move between places or countries? What is the general pattern of these movements and how are they determined?

Here, a system has been defined as a complex of interacting elements, together with their attributes and relationships. One of the major tasks in conceptualizing a migration phenomenon as a system is to identify the basic interacting elements of migration and their attributes and relationships. Once this is done, it soon becomes obvious that the migration system operates not in a void but in a special environment. This environment comprises "the set of all objects a change in whose attributes affects the system, and also those objects whose attributes are changed by the behavior of the system."[32]

The environment within which the system of migration operates is created by 'conditions of insecurity' at origin and 'conditions of secured life' at destination. The breakdown of security within an orbit sharpens the

32 For details see, Akin L. Mabogunje, "Systems Approach to a Theory of Rural-Urban Migration," in Robin Cohen (ed.), *Theories of Migration,* (Cheltenham: Edward Elgar Publishing Ltd., 1996), pp. 44-58.

peoples' stimuli to move. The basic interacting elements to be identified in a system of migration are:[33]

1. A stimuli from environment by which a migrant decides to move.
2. A variety of information which creates 'propensity to migrate' or what is called 'migration elasticity' being transmitted to a migrant before he makes the desired move.
3. Within a migration system framework, attention is focused not only on the migrant but also on the various institutions (sender and receiver states and governments or sub-systems such as rural and urban administrations) and the political, social, economic, and other relationships (adjustment mechanisms in the new place of resettlement) which are the integral part of the broader migration process of transformation.
4. A control system or a sub-control system which supervises the operation of the general system and determines when and how to increase or decrease the amount of flows into the system just like a *thermostat* controls the amount of heat that flows into a given area. A control system may include: a family, a community, a collectivity of groups, national and local administrations, and also various socio-political organizations at different locations both within and outside a country.
5. A migration system comprises not only matter (the migrant, the institutions, and various organizations mentioned) but also energy. In the physical sense, energy, particularly "potential energy" is the body's capacity of doing work by

33 *Ibid.*, pp. 46-58.

virtue of "stresses" resulting from its relation either with its environment or with other bodies. This potential energy likened to the stimuli acts on individuals to move. Unlike push and pull theory which suggest that people migrate for minus (–) and plus (+) factors, for example, environmental deterioration as minus (–) factor push people out and plus (+) factor like better and secured life elsewhere pull people out, the migration systems theory, in contrast, suggests that people migrate for differential individual responses to the stimuli derived both from the environment and from within the system. People move for a set of plausible reasons and not at a simple negative and positive level as explained by push and pull approach.

6. As soon as an individual moves from one place to another, his role in the system is greatly amplified. Basic to an understanding of this amplified role is the concept of "information," a central notion in the theory of communications. Information in a system is defined as bits of messages which lead to a set of actions. Thus, it is assumed that a migrant soon starts to transmit back to his origin information about his reception and status in the new place of resettlement.

7. Of equal importance is the notion of "feedback" which has been the focus of the field of Cybernetics. The migration systems theory explains its feedback mechanism in terms of stimulus-response behavior. A stimulus affects a receptor which communicates this message to some controlling apparatus and from this to an affecter which gives the response. In feedback,

the affecter's activity is monitored back to the receptor with the result that the system's behavior is in some way modified by the information. The feedback process has one of the two effects. It can further amplify the deviation (in this case by stimulating further migration), or it may counteract the deviation by encouraging a return to the initial situation. Deviation-amplifying feedbacks are regarded as positive; deviation-counteracting feedbacks as negative. The general experience is that migrants are never lost to their origin but continue to send back information.

8. Within a migration system framework, it is assumed that one of the concomitants of the continued interaction between the system and its environment will be the phenomenon of growth in the system. This phenomenon involves more than a simple growth or increase in the number of people moving from one area to another. It is much more complex, involving not only the individual components of the system but also the interaction between them and the system as a whole.

9. The interaction between migrants and the system in effect modifies the character of politics, economy, population, and society within any given destination country. The feedback role of migration between origin and destination transforms both areas through the information exchange.

The migration systems theory enables us to explain migration not as a linear, uni-directional, push and pull, cause-effect movement, but as a circular, interdependent, progressively complex, and self-modifying system in which the effect of changes in one part can be traced through the whole of the system. According to this theory, migration is a continuous spatial process shaping the human occupancy of the earth's surface.

World Systems Theory of Migration

In world systems theory, political scientists examine migration in a framework of global political system as economists would do it in a framework of global economic system.[34] According to global political system framework, migration is an integral part of the world political system created through the expansion of European empire. The leading explainers of this approach are Hannah Arendt and Aristide Zolberg, both political scientists, who have assessed the fact that migration, particularly contemporary refugee flows are rooted in the breakdown of the European colonies across the globe. As asserted by them, the process of decolonization and the increasing number of nation states after 1945 contributed to the generation of massive refugee migration flows. Unlike general population migration which is patterned by economic factors, these refugee flows are patterned by political forces such as civil strife, abrupt changes of regime, arbitrary government decision and international war, all of which are usually considered singular and unpredictable occurrences. These forces are said to be the manifestations of political trends that are much likely to surface in the contemporary world. Refugee migration flows are a concomitant of world-politics as ordinary migration is of world-economics.[35]

It has been emphasized in this framework that the notion of "political persecution" is crucial because it helps

34 Ronald Skeldon, n. 26, p. 24.

35 For details see, Aristide R. Zolberg, 'The Formation of New States as a Refugee-Generating Process,' in Robin Cohen (ed.), *Theories of Migration,* (Cheltenham: Edward Elgar Publishing Ltd., 1996), pp. 282-296.

one distinguish victims that include most of the citizens of illiberal states, be these totalitarian or authoritarian, that is, a large part of the world's population who are singled out as targets of the willful exercise of extraordinary malevolence on the part of the agent. Further, the notion is important because it helps us trace how states select certain categories of population as targets of persecution, expelling them outright or creating conditions that provoke them into risky flights.[36]

Hannah Arendt's analysis show how the dissolution of Europe's erstwhile multinational empires as those of Russia and Austria-Hungary created multiple new states "in the image of nation-states" leading to the reduction of traditional secular and human rights doctrines of the West. The working of these newly nation-states implied only nationals can be citizens, only people of same national origin can enjoy the full protection of legal institutions whereas persons of different nationality needed some law of exception until or unless they were completely assimilated and divorced from their origin. The nation state-formula was adopted to organize political life in regions containing ethnically mixed population, often intractably interspersed across geographical space that it proved impossible to constitute homogenous political entities of viable size. The yawning gap between the formula and social realities generated enormous tensions, out of which two victim groups emerged. They were the minorities and the stateless that lost those rights which had been defined as inalienable, namely the Rights of Man. Minorities had existed before having enjoyed secular tradition and all human rights, but since the creation of newly nation-states they had been turned into political misfits. Such political dynamic of nation-states created refugee-producing conditions in Europe. Theoretically, the concept

36 *Ibid.*, p. 283.

of sovereignty is nowhere more absolute than in matters of emigration, nationality and expulsion.[37]

In analogous vein, Zolberg has emphasized that an analysis of the historical processes of democratic revolutions such as the French and American revolutions since the late eighteenth century provides the principal key for understanding how refugees come about. The model of nation-state comprised a social and a cultural content ever since the age of the democratic revolutions. This social and cultural content is the underlying force for the creation of refugees. For example, the nation-state of France that had emerged out of democratic revolution generated cultural refugees known as the aristocratic émigrés. The newly nation-states formed out of the debris of empires inherited the legacy. Cultural minorities are viewed as obstacles to successful nation building process. The massive contemporary refugee flows are most prominently concomitant of transformation of world empires and of small self-sufficient communities or tribes into a world of national states.[38]

Further, the emergence of new states throughout Asia and Africa triggered within each of them "integrative revolution" which required destruction of old solidarities as well as the fostering of new ones. Formation of nation-states out of sharply divided societies as encountered in most of the contemporary third world would generate political tension. The intrinsic difficulties of the task are compounded by underdevelopment. Underdevelopment contributes to the generation of refugee flows in that it fosters the adoption of authoritarian strategies of state and nation formation, whose execution entails political persecution of certain categories of the population. It is generally evident that groups like ethnic minorities that

---

37 *Ibid.,* p. 286.

38 *Ibid.,* p. 288.

straddle more than one state; trading diasporas without homeland; ethnic groups associated with colonial rule as indigenous governing classes; any victims who seek to defend themselves and hence, by definition, come to be tagged as subversive. Since the integrative revolution tended to erupt in the wake of decolonization, many of the potential refugee flows associated with the formation of new states in Asia and Africa have already occurred like the Chakma exodus to Arunachal Pradesh.

Transition Theory of Migration

Transition theory hypothesizes migration as a lever of change and evolution. The theory suggests that migration brings transition such as from a primarily tribal society to a primarily modern society (the social transition), from a high mortality society to low a mortality society (the demographic transition), from an agricultural economy to industrial economy (economic transition), and from an apolitical society to a political society (political transition).[39] Political transition theory to the study of international migration has been emphasized by scholars like Myron Weiner, Stephen Castles and Mark J. Miller.

Weiner describes international migration as a political force and migrants as political actors causing change in political processes of the country in which migrants reside and in the relationship between their country of residence and their country of origin. He provides two propositions for political transition. His first proposition is that migrants, or their descendants, seek to alter migration policies in their country of residence intended to benefit economic and political rights. To gain such objectives, migrants attempt to promote various political interventions. He demonstrated these variations by

39 Ronald Skeldon, n. 27, pp. 31-32.

referring to: Sikh secessionists in the United Kingdom; immigrant Filipino opponents of President Marcos in the United States; Polish immigrants and their descendants in Chicago; immigrants from Timor in Holland. Migrants invariably seek to recreate their own religious, social and cultural institutions. Where permitted they often develop their own media, schools for their children, religious institutions and political organizations.[40]

Weiner's second proposition is that migration is critical because it brings transition in politics and economy within a given space. The fear of migrants turns the local people to be protective of their political space and economic opportunities that exist within it. Under such situation when migrants seek expansion of their political and economic opportunities within that space, it results in intense conflicts between the immigrant residents and the local population for control over political and economic resources and opportunities, political power and social status. This proposition of Weiner's also suggests that migration brings changes in the activities of various socio-political organizations, particularly in relation to electoral politics within that given space. For example, political parties draw political capital out of migration problem. He emphasizes that migration contributes to understanding the size, composition, and distribution of population in relation to both government and politics, and also the political determinants and political consequences of population change.[41]

---

40 Myron Weiner, 'On International Migration and International Relations,' in Robin Cohen (ed.), *Theories of Migration*, (Cheltenham: Edward Elgar Publishing Ltd., 1996), pp. 306-7.

41 Myron Weiner, *Sons of the Soil: Migration and Ethnic Conflict in India*, (Princeton: Princeton University Press, 1978), pp. 3-4.

Castles and Miller provide a four-stage transition model that explains the migration from Mediterranean countries to Western Europe and to Australia, and from Latin America and Asia to North America. This model provides a framework for the assessment of international migration purely on normative basis. The four stages in the development of an international migration system are postulated as follows:

- **Stage 1**: temporary labor migration of young workers, remittance of earning and continued orientation to the homeland;
- **Stage 2**: prolonging of stay and the development of social networks based on kinship or common area of origin and the need for mutual help in the new environment;
- **Stage 3**: family reunion, growing consciousness of long-term settlement, increasing orientation towards the receiving country, and emergence of ethnic communities with their own institutions (associations, shops, agencies, professions);
- **Stage 4**: permanent settlement which, depending on the policies of the government and the behavior of the population of the receiving country, leads either to secure legal status and eventual citizenship, or to political exclusion, socio-economic marginalization and the formation of permanent ethnic minorities.[42]

Castles and Miller suggest that international migration evolves in stages driven by an intrinsic momentum in the migration process. The fourth stage conjures up that there is a changing relationship between migration and political transition in the receiving country.

---

42 Stephen Castles and Mark J. Miller, n. 19, p. 25.

Political Consequences of Migration

Although it is important to discuss the factors, meaning, types and theories of migration for this study, it is also significant here to discuss the political outcomes and consequences of migration. The above transition theory of migration suggests that migration is a potential political factor. Migration is not simply the transfer of people from one place of residence to another but also an important component for understanding the ever changing "political patterns" and "political relations" of an area.[43] As stated in the *Encyclopaedia Britannica*: "Human migrations within recorded history have transformed the political aspect of all continents."[44]

Migration causes formation of new political set up both at origin and destination. Migration not only brings intense interactions between different societies but also qualitative changes in political patterns often leading to violent conflicts between different groups.[45] Whatever may be the cause and distance of migration, it invariably ends up in the transformation of political structures of both the place of its origin and the place of reception. As a result, the nature of politics both at origin and at destination usually does not stay the same. Migration affects both national and international political life.

Causes of Chakma Migration to Arunachal Pradesh

On the question of the causes of migration and resettlement, 20 percent respondents said it was due to persecution policy of the Pakistan Government, 68

---

43 W. A. V. Clark, n. 17, p. 24.

44 *The Encyclopaedia Britannica,* Vol. 6, (London: Encyclopaedia Britannica Inc., 1998), p. 137.

45 U. Schuerkens, "Transnational Migrations and Social Transformations: A Theoretical Perspective," in *Current Sociology*, Vol. 53, No. 4, Monograph 2, July, 2005, p. 539.

percent said that it was due to displacement while 12 percent said it was due to both persecution and displacement. Thus, the Chakma exodus to Arunachal Pradesh was caused by two different circumstances: 1) Pakistan government's persecution policy over the Chakmas and 2) Kaptai Dam and Displacement of the Chakmas.

Pakistan government's persecution policy over the Chakmas

The Chakmas are an indigenous tribal community of the Chittagong Hill Tracts (CHT) of former East Pakistan, now Bangladesh. They differed from the majority people of Pakistan in three respects: they are the Sino-Tibetan descent; their language is more akin to those spoken by their neighbors in North-East India and Burma; and they are predominantly Buddhist. During partition of British India, a delegation of the Chakmas went to Delhi and demanded that the CHT be included in India. Nehru and Patel assured the delegation that the CHT would be included in India. With the belief that the CHT had been included in India, the CHT leaders hoisted the Indian flag in the Deputy Commissioner's office at Rangamati on August 15, 1947, the 'Appointed Day of Indian Independence.' It is said that the Deputy Commissioner of the district of CHT, G. L. Hyde himself agreed that thc CHT became free at that very moment as a part and parcel of free India.[46] But to the surprise of the CHT people, on August 17, 1947, the Boundary Commission announced that the CHT was included in Pakistan. On August 21, 1947 the Pakistan Government took over the CHT. In 1964, the government of Pakistan ended the special status of the CHT followed by its persecution policy over the Chakmas

46 For details see, "Partition Potentials," *The Telescope*, Agartala, June 11, 1975, p. 1-3.

because they expressed anti-Pakistani sentiment during the partition. The victims were forced to leave for India.[47]

Kaptai Dam and Displacement of the Chakmas

It was in the Pakistan period in 1964 that the massive Kaptai hydro-electric dam was built in the CHT leading to the creation of a huge reservoir which displaced an estimated 100,000 Chakmas from their lands and livelihoods. About 40,000 of these displaced Chakmas came to India, majority of whom went to the NEFA.[48]

The Kaptaidam was built across the Karnafuli River in the village of Kaptai (27 kilometer west of Rangamati town) with a bilateral loan from the United States Agency for International Development (USAID).[49] The government of Pakistan undertook the construction project of the dam in 1959 and completed in 1963. It had catastrophic consequences for the Chakmas leading to the widespread disruption of their traditional socio-cultural, political, economic and environmental system. The huge reservoir created by the dam flooded an area of 1,036 square kilometer, covering the entire Karnafuli river valley lands and its tributaries in which 21,853 hectares (40 percent of best agricultural lands in the CHT) were plough lands and the rests were *swidden* lands, fruit gardens, administrative centers, trading and

---

47 Myron Weiner, 'Rejected Peoples and Unwanted Migrants in South Asia', in *Economic and Political Weekly*, Vol. 28, No. 34, Mumbai, August 21, 1993, pp. 1737-1746.

48 Chittagong Hill Tracts Commission, *Life is Not Ours: Land and Human Rights in the Chittagong Hill Tracts, Bangladesh,'* (Copenhagen, Amsterdam: International Work Group for Indigenous Affairs (IWGIA), Organizing Committee Chittagong Hill Tracts Campaign, May 1991), p. 13.

49 Government of Bangladesh, *Bangladesh District Gazetteers: Chittagong Hill Tracts,* (Dacca: Government Press, 1971), p. 155.

market places, homesteads, government forest reserves, and so on.[50]

As a result, the Chakmas had lost their lands, homes, means of subsistence and virtually everything that they had before the flooding of the area. Adam Curle, one of the engineers engaged with the dam project remarked:

> The people who had been affected were mostly Buddhist tribe of the Chakmas and had been totally dispossessed of their agricultural fields...The once close-knit society and culture had been fragmented forever.[51]

According to Anti-Slavery Society, the victims were promised both financial compensation and substitute land. However, most of them are said have received no compensation of any kind.[52] In consequence, a large number of them migrated to India. They entered India through Tripura and the Lushai Hill District (now Mizoram). On arrival, they were first given temporary shelter in Tripura and in the Lushai Hills. Then the Central Government of India offered them a choice of locations for future resettlement which included NEFA and Bihar. The choice fell on NEFA. It was reported in some newspapers that the choice of NEFA by the Chakmas suited the Government of India and its numerous security agencies in the region for at least two reasons. Firstly, the Chakmas were Buddhist and were expected to get along well with their immediate

---

50 Aditya Kumar Dewan, *Class and Ethnicity in the Chittagong Hill Tracts of Southeastern Bangladesh*, ((PhD thesis, submitted in McGill University, Canada, 1991), p. 226.

51 Adam Curle, *Making Peace*, (London: Tavistock Publication, 1971), p. 101.

52 Anti Slavery Society, *Chittagong Hill Tracts: Militarization, Oppression and the Hill Tribes,* (London: Anti Slavery Society, 1984), p. 32.

neighbors and co-religionists, the Singphos and Khamtis. Secondly, the Chakmas were seen as another community to buttress the Indian security presence, especially after the 1962 war with China when Chinese troops sliced through NEFA like a knife through butter.[53]

After being informed of Chakmas' decision to go to NEFA, Mr. Mahabir Tyagi, the then Rehabilitation Minister immediately flew to Shillong in order to direct special trains from Guwahati for transporting the Chakmas to NEFA, particularly those flowing through Aizawl. Those flowing through Tripura are said to have started their journey for NEFA with the help of local Chakma guides. They were asked to halt and regroup at Ledo and Margherita, the entry points to NEFA. In the mean time, Chakmas from the Manchera Transit camp in Assam also reached Ledo. Those who were taken to Bihar were also redirected to NEFA via Ledo. It was towards the end of 1964 that Chakmas were allowed to enter NEFA territory by the NEFA administration and then they were taken to Namphai village where they camped out until the government rehabilitation program began in certain specified areas.[54]

Resettlement of the Chakmas in Arunachal Pradesh

According to the opinions of Chakma respondents who have been interviewed for the purpose this study, they were resettled in demarcated areas of Miao Sub-division (Diyun Circle) of the Changlang District, Chowkham Circle of the Lohit District and Kokila Circle of the Papumpare District under a special scheme by the Central Government of India on the basis of their

53 For details see, "The Chakmas' flight to nowhere," *The Indian Express,* New Delhi, October 17, 1994.

54 For details see, "Partition Potentials," n. 46, p. 1-3.

'Relief Eligibility Certificates.' The opinions of the respondents are consistent with a letter issued by the Ministry of Home Affairs.[55]

Since NEFA was then administered by the President of India through the Governor of Assam under the general supervision and control of the Ministry of External Affairs, the question of relief and rehabilitation of the Chakmas fell upon the discretion of Central Rehabilitation Department of India.[56] Accordingly, the Central Government endorsed a detailed scheme for their rehabilitation in consultation with the Governor's administration in NEFA as well as by an agreement with the concerned local headmen and land owners.[57] The scheme was structured in conformity with the general rules of Government rehabilitation, that is, Chakmas would be provided relief and rehabilitation on the basis of their camp registration certificate known as 'Relief Eligibility Certificate' containing particulars of the migrant.

Under the scheme, each Chakma family was allotted land varying from 5 to 10 acres depending upon the size of the family in addition to a rehabilitation grant of Rs. 4,200 per family. The Central Government was reported to have spent a total of Rs. 130.41 lakhs (Rs.1,341

---

55 Letter D. O. No. 12/16/92/-MZ, Minister of State for Home and Parliamentary Affairs, India, North Block, New Delhi, September 23, 1992, .

56 According to the Constitution of India, 'relief and rehabilitation' of refugees is to be undertaken by the State with full or partial financial support from the Center. In the Indian Union, the question of relief and rehabilitation of refugees is enshrined as a state subject. As NEFA was controlled by the Ministry of External Affairs till 1965, the rehabilitation question of the Chakmas in 1964 fell upon the Central discretion.

57 Rajya Sabha Committee on Petitions, *Hundred and Fifth Report*, (New Delhi: Rajya Sabha Secretariat, 14 August, 1997), pp. 43-44.

thousand) between 1964 and 1968, when it had transferred the scheme to the NEFA Administration for further implementation.[58] As stated by S. P. Talukdar:

> Chakmas were permanently absorbed in the state of Arunachal Pradesh in 1964 by an agreement between the traditional leaders of the state and the Central Government of India and thereafter the Chakmas started new life and built a new society as ordained by fate.[59]

As a part of further implementation of the scheme, the NEFA administration is said to have issued trade licenses and ration cards to the Chakmas and provided employment, and education and medical facilities. Given that, Chakmas recreated their own social and economic institutions. Social institutions included, for example, Chakma Panchayat composed of a number of village committees, each headed by a *Murubbi* (headman). Economic institutions included markets of their own in which they sought to establish shops with official license numbers and sold rice, cattle, jute and variety of vegetables to buyers from short and long distances. Many Chakmas are said to have learnt to write and speak Assamese and Hindi. That reflected the socio-economic absorption of the Chakams in Arunachal Pradesh.[60] In

58 Rajya Sabha Committee on Petitions, n. 57, pp. 43-44.

59 S. P. Talukdar, *The Chakmas Life and Struggle*, (Delhi: Gyan Publishing House, 1988), pp. 101-104.

60 Based on an interview with a Chakma headman, aged about 65, who runs a grocery and garment shop at Diyun market with license number DYN-26/79. According to him, in 1979, 23 trade licenses were issued to the Chakmas settled in Diyun Circle, Changlang District of which he held one.

1965, NEFA was brought under the control of the Ministry of Home Affairs.[61]

According to the Ministry of Home Affairs, there was no opposition from the local population to the settlement of the Chakmas. Chakmas are reported to have lived amicably with their immediate neighbors like the Singphos and Khamtis in Diyun and Bordumsa Circles in Changlang District, with the Nishis and Apatanis in Balijan Circle in present Papumpare District. The same was maintained with the Kamptis in Chowkham Circle in Lohit District. However, the local tribals started resenting the presence of the Chakmas due to encroachment by them on lands outside original settlements. The fact that Chakmas had developed original forest land into agricultural fields conducive to both food and cash crop farming also became a source of envy.[62] Further, the growing population of the Chakmas created demographic threat in the minds of the smaller native groups such as the Singphos.[63] The

61 The NEFA has undergone a series of administrative reorganization since 1947. From 1947-1949, it was administered by the Governor of Assam acting on the Provincial Ministry. From 1950-1964, it was administered by the President of India through the Governor of Assam under the supervision of the Ministry of External Affairs. From 1965-70, it was administered as before by the Governor of Assam as agent of the President but under the general supervision and control of the Ministry of Home Affairs. In 1971, it became Union Territory of Arunachal Pradesh. On February 20, 1987, Arunachal Pradesh graduated to full-fledged Statehood. For details see, P. N. Luthra, *Constitutional and Administrative Growth of the NEFA,* (Shillong: NEFA, 1971), p. 42.

62 Rajya Sabha Committee on Petition, n. 57, p. 44.

63 "The Chakmas' flight to nowhere," n. 53.

present population of the Chakmas numbers about 40,000.[64]

However, since 1992 Arunachal Pradesh has become a site of problem with the various native socio-political organizations spearheading movement against the Chakma refugees as reported by most local and national newspapers. The problem has not only drawn the attention of the state Assembly of Arunachal Pradesh and the national Parliament of India but also the National Human Rights Commission of India and academic researchers at large. The whole issue centers on the question of citizenship of the Chakmas in Arunachal Pradesh. The issue became complex as it relates not only to the citizenship question of the Chakmas who actually migrated but also the Chakmas who are born within the state of Arunachal Pradesh during last half a century.

Methodology

Data for the study have been collected through both primary and secondary sources. Primary sources included the proceedings of the Arunachal Pradesh Legislative Assembly and Parliamentary debates, records and publications of the Government of Arunachal Pradesh, the Central Government of India, reports of the Rajya

---

64 The available data on the present population of the Chakmas in Arunachal Pradesh are conflicting. The census of 1981 put the figure at 16,018. After 1981, no census report is available on Chakmas in Arunachal Pradesh. In 1994, the Chief Minister, Gegong Apang gave an official figure of the Chakma population as 35,000. The newspaper reports put it between 45,000 and 65,000. The figure 40,000 as presented here has been obtained from the Chakma *Murubbis* (Chakma Village Panchyat Heads) in Arunachal Pradesh and is found to be consistent with the registration books maintained by the Chakma Panchayats in Arunachal Pradesh.

Sabha Committee on Petitions, National Human Rights Commission of India (NHRC, Delhi), Judgment of the Supreme Court of India (New Delhi, 1996) and Judgment of the Gauhati High Court (Gauhati, Assam, 1994). It also included the publications of the AAPSU, the Organizing Committee Peoples' Referendum Rally (Naharlagun, Arunachal Pradesh), various political parties in Arunachal Pradesh, the Delhi Chakma Students' Union (DCSU), the Committee for Citizenship Rights of the Chakmas of Arunachal Pradesh (CCRCAP, New Delhi), the All Arunachal Pradesh Chakma Youths' Federation (Diyun, Arunachal Pradesh), reports of the Peoples' Rights Organization (PRO, New Delhi), publications of the Humanity Protection Forum (HPF, Agartala, Tripura), the All India Chakma Cultural Conference (AICCC, Machmara, Tripura), newsletters published by the Chakma Rights and Development Organization (CRDO, Bangalore), publications of the Joint-Action-Committee (JAC, Diyun, Arunachal Pradesh), the Amnesty International (London, UK), the Organizing Committee Chittagong Hill Tracts Campaign (Amsterdam, The Netherlands), the International Work Group for Indigenous Affairs (IWGIA, Copenhagen, Denmark), the Survival International (London, UK), memoranda, appeals of various organizations, letters and recommendations of the Members of Indian Parliament and local newspaper accounts.

Primary sources also included the data collected through structured and unstructured interviews with a cross section of the Chakmas in three districts of Arunachal Pradesh namely, the Lower Subansiri, the Changlang and the Lohit, where the Chakmas are concentrated. In view of an estimated Chakma population of about 40,000,a stratified random sample of 150 has been proportionately drawn from each of the three districts depending on their population size obtained from the village heads. The stratification has been done on the basis of sex, deriving a male and a female from alternate households. Some existing and former General Secretaries of the AAPSU, the DCSU, the CCRCAP, and district officials like Deputy Collectors, political leaders like Members of Parliament and Members of Legislative Assembly, NGO leaders, and some Chakma leaders like Panchayat and Village Headmen have also been interviewed. Primary data has also been collected from census reports, statistical hand books, published and unpublished research works.

Secondary sources included data collected from books and articles published in various journals and newspapers.

Data collected through both primary and secondary sources have been cross-checked, tabulated and analyzed on qualitative basis. These data have been used throughout the text of the study and then major findings have been drawn.

CHAPTER - II

Chakma Issue and the All Arunachal Pradesh Students' Union (AAPSU)

The history of AAPSU movement on the Chakma issue dates back to the early 1980s. The year 1979 is marked as a turning point in the history of the AAPSU because it was that year when the AAPSU for the first time made a drastic shift from its earlier peaceful strategy of 'prayer, petition and partnership with the Government' to agitational mode mainly in response to the Chakma issue and some boundary disputes with Assam which was reported to have created "apprehension and anger" in the minds of the students of Arunachal Pradesh.[1] In the same year, the All Assam Students' Union (AASU) launched an intensive movement against the illegal foreign nationals in Assam. In 1980, the AASU

1 For details see, S. Dutta, 'Student Movement in Arunachal Pradesh,' in A. K. Baruah (ed.), *Student Power in North-East India Understanding Student Movements,* (New Delhi: Regency Publications, 2002), pp. 209-14.

set an agitational programme to compel the government to identify and expel the 'illegal foreign nationals' from Assam.[2] Since Arunachal Pradesh has also been affected by resettlement of foreign nationals such as Chakma, Hajong and Tibetan refugees, the Assam agitation on the foreign national issue is reported to have influenced the AAPSU to launch a similar movement against the Chakma, Hajong and Tibetan refugees in Arunachal Pradesh.[3] It has been reflected when the AAPSU launched its movement in 1982 under the leadership of Jarban Gamlin, the then President of the AAPSU, inter alia, demanding the deportation of Chakma, Hajong and Tibetan refugees from Arunachal Pradesh. It was at that stage that the Chakma issue started to figure prominently in the programmes of the AAPSU.

Factors responsible for AAPSU Movement on the Chakma issue

The AAPSU movement in response to the Chakma issue was conditioned by different external and internal factors. The external factors include inspiration from the Assam movement and the North East Students Organization (NESO). The internal factors include rapid expansion of education in Arunachal Pradesh, pessimism over government's failure to resolve the Chakma issue, demographic and political threat of the Chakmas, feeling of exclusiveness with the Inner Line Regulation Act 1873, and strategic location. These conditioning factors are examined hereunder.

---

2 For details see, Prafulla Kumar Mahanta, *The Tussle between the Citizens and Foreigners in Assam*, (Sahidabad: Vikas Publishing House, 1986), pp. 4-15.

3 S. Dutta, n. 1, p. 209.

External factors

Inspiration from the Assam Movement

The Assam Movement (or Assam Agitation) was a popular movement against undocumented migrants in Assam between 1979 and 1985. The Assam Movement originated in 1978 when the member of the Lok Sabha, Hiralal Patwari, died necessitating a by-election in the Mangaldoi Lok Sabha Constituency. During the process of the election it was identified that the electorate had grown phenomenally because of inclusion of foreign national voters. As a result, the AASU demanded that the elections be postponed till the names of 'foreign nationals' are deleted from the electoral rolls leading to the birth of Assam Agitation. It is regarded as one of the most vibrant democratic mass movements of independent India. The movement, led by the AASU and the All Assam Gana Sangram Parishad (AAGSP), set an agitational programme to compel the government to identify and expel the 'illegal foreign nationals' in Assam. Although the agitational programmes of the AASU were non-violent, there were incidents of violence, like the Nellie Massacre. The AASU agitation ended on August 15, 1985 following the Assam Accord that was signed between the agitation leaders and the Government of India.[4]

According to the opinion of non-Chakma respondents, the Assam movement had been a great source of inspiration for the AAPSU to launch its movement against the Chakma refugees in Arunachal Pradesh. It has been evident from AAPSU's identical agitational programmes against Chakmas in Arunachal Pradesh with AASU's agitational programmes against foreign nationals in Assam. The Assam Accord of August 15,

---

4 For details see, Prafulla Kumar Mahanta, n. 2, pp.4-15.

1985 is said to have further encouraged the AAPSU to launch intense agitation against the Chakmas.[5]

Inspiration from North East Students' Organization (NESO)

NESO is the umbrella organization of various students' unions of all the seven states of North East India. Besides its demand for rapid economic development of North East India, it also demands detection and deportation of illegal foreign nationals from the region.[6]

Table 2.1 Population of Students in different States of North East India by 1991

State	Population	Students High School and Above	%age of Students School and Above
Arunachal Pradesh	8,64,558	21,890	2.53
Assam	224,14,322	7,60,520	3.40
Manipur	18,37,149	92,399	5.02
Meghalaya	17,75,778	67,039	3.77
Mizoram	6,89,756	28,096	4.07
Nagaland	12,09,546	30,239	2.50
Tripura	27,57,205	85,706	3.10

Source: Compiled from *Census of India,* 1991; A. K. Baruah (ed.), *Student Power in North-East India Understanding Student Movements,* (New Delhi: Regency Publications, 2002), p. 3.

On August 15, 1995, the NESO called an eleven-hour *bandh* in protest of Centre's step-motherly attitude towards the North East India and demanded detection and deportation of 'foreign nationals' from the region.

---

5 S. Dutta, n. 1, p. 211.

6 *Ibid.,* p. 219.

7 *Ibid.,* p. 220.

Since NESO launched movement on the issue of 'foreign nationals' in the region, it reinforced the inspiration of the AAPSU to launch agitation against the Chakmas in Arunachal Pradesh. This had been evident from the participation of the AAPSU in the *bandh* called by NESO on August 15, 1995 with 150 students under the leadership of Domin Loya.[7] According to Table 2.1, the student population of Arunachal Pradesh in 1991 stood at 21,890 out of the total population of the State 8,64,558 in 1991.

Internal factors

Rapid expansion of education in Arunachal Pradesh

Rapid expansion of education in Arunachal Pradesh since the early 1980s gave rise to a group of educated elites who were determined to stand and fight against those forces that are seen to have threatened the territorial, social, demographic and political integrity of Arunachal Pradesh.[8] In 1947, there were only four primary schools in the NEFA. At the end of the Seventh Plan (1989-1990), the number of educational institutions in Arunachal Pradesh had risen to a total of 1705, followed by 1845 in 1990-91, 1987 in 1991-92, and 2157 in 1992-93.[9] As a result, the rate of literacy also increased.

Further, as per census reports, the literacy rate in the state stood at 7.23 percent in 1961, at 11.29 percent in 1971, at 20.79 percent in 1981, and at 41.59 percent in 1991.[10] In 1991 Arunachal Pradesh had acquired an estimated 21,890 student population in high schools,

---

8 For details see, Preamble to the Constitution of the AAPSU, website:*aapsu.org/constitution.php.*

9 For details see, Table 2.1 which shows the growth in the number of educational institutions in Arunachal Pradesh from 1989-1993.

10 For details see, Census of India, 1961, 1971, 1981, 1991.

Table 2.2 Growth of Enrolment in Schools ('000) from 1990-1993 in Arunachal Pradesh

Stages	1990-1991	1991-1992	1992-1993	% increase 1991-1992 over 1990-1991	in 1991-1993 over 1991-1992
1. Pre-Primary	13	15	16	15.38	6.67
2. Elementary (I-VIII)	138	147	154	6.52	4.76
3. Secondary Class	11	12	13	9.09	8.33
4. Hr. Secy.	5	5	6	—	20.00
5. Graduate	1	2	3	100.00	50.00
6. Post Graduate	.1	.1	.2	—	6.13
(a) Total enrolment	168.1	181.1	192.2	7.73	6.13
(b) Enrolment of students belonging to Arunachal Pracesh Scheduled Tribe (APST)	119	129	141	8.40	9.30
(c) % of APST enrolment to total enrolment	71%	71%	73%		

Source: *Economic Review of Arunachal Pradesh,* 1993, Directorate of Economics and Statistics, Government of Arunachal Pradesh, Itanagar.

colleges and universities.[11] Table 2.2 shows growth of enrolment of students from 1990 to 1993 while Table 2.3 shows expansion of educational institutions in Arunachal Pradesh between 1989 and 1993.

Social Obligation

Like any other active social agents, the AAPSU also believes in the fact that it is a social obligation on its part to engage itself in movement against threats from foreign nationals as it is committed to 'preserve and safeguard the culture, customs, traditional heritages, and the territory' of Arunachal Pradesh.[12] The socio-administrative structure of Arunachal Pradesh provided ample democratic space for the student community of the State to participate in community affairs and services. The authorities in administration also utilized the services of the student community. The absence of political parties in the State till 1977 further provided opportunities to the students to mediate with the Government for various social, educational and developmental issues. However, the administration of Arunachal Pradesh was not vocal about the Chakma issue. Thus, the AAPSU leaders thought that it was their responsibility to demand for the deportation of the Chakma refugees from Arunachal Pradesh.[13]

Pessimism over the Future of the Chakma Issue

For resolving the Chakma issue amicably, the AAPSU submitted several memoranda to the Government of

---

11 For details see, Census of India, 1991.

12 Preamble to the Constitution of the AAPSU, n. 8, website:*aapsu.org/constitution.php.*

13 For details see, J. N. Chowdhury, "The People of Arunachal Pradesh," *Arunachal Panorama,* (Directorate of Research, Itanagar, 1992), pp. 37-150.

Table 2.3 Growth of Educational Institutions in Arunachal Pradesh from 1989 to1993

Sl. No.	Educational Institutions	1989-1990	1990-1991	1991-1992	1992-1993
1.	Pre-Primary Schools	249	249	284	299
2.	Primary Schools	1,101	1,122	1,144	1,174
3.	Middle School	236	250	265	274
4.	Secondary Schools	68	73	78	84
5.	Hr. Secondary Schools	45	46	49	54
6.	College	4	4	4	4
7.	University	1	1	1	1
	Total	*1,704*	*1,745*	*1,825*	*1,890*
8.	Community Schools	1	100	162	266
	Total	*1,705*	*1,845*	*1,987*	*2,156*

Source: *Economic Review of Arunachal Pradesh,* Directorate of Economics and Statistics, Government of Arunachal Pradesh, Itanagar, 1993.

Arunachal Pradesh, but were of no avail. Government's failure to resolve the Chakma issue cast an air of deep pessimism over the future of the Chakma issue. As a result, after detailed deliberations in a three-day general meeting held from July 15 to 17, 1986, the AAPSU submitted an Ultimatum to the Government of Arunachal Pradesh to resolve the refugee problem within the month of September 1986 failing which the AAPSU "will be left with no other alternative but to take agitational path."[14] After receiving the Ultimatum, the then Chief Minister of Arunachal Pradesh, Gegong Apang, promised the AAPSU President Naban Rabia and its General Secretary, Tabin Taki that the Government of Arunachal Pradesh would soon send a delegation to New Delhi to request the Centre for taking immediate measures to deport the Chakmas from Arunachal Pradesh. There was no positive response from the Centre to deport the Chakmas of Arunachal Pradesh.

Demographic and Political Threats

What led the AAPSU to resort to agitational path is also linked to the demographic and political threats posed by the Chakmas. It is often alleged by the AAPSU, as its resolution passed on August 26, 1985, shows, that "in certain areas the concentration of Chakma refugees and speedy growth of their population has threatened to change the demographic picture of the area." The demand for citizenship rights by the Chakmas also created a political fear in the minds of the Arunachalis as the Organizing Committee Peoples Referendum Rally of Arunachal Pradesh alleged.[15]

---

14 For details see, Memo No. AAPSU/GS-18/01 dated August 1, 1986, Itanagar.

15 Organising Committee Peoples' Referendum Rally, *An Appeal*, Naharlagun, Arunachal Pradesh, September 20, 1995.

Fear of Land Alienation

The AAPSU also alleged that the demand of permanent settlement of the Chakmas in the districts of Lower Subansiri, Changlang and Lohit and their preparation of a map to strengthen their claims have created tensions among the Arunachalese. The AAPSU further alleged that a considerable segment of the Chakmas have encroached into the forest land beyond their demarcated areas and many a time they have been evicted by the police from those encroached areas which has created a fear of land alienation in the minds of the Arunachalis. The AAPSU asserts that its movement against the Chakmas is to protect their right to land, forest and water resources in Arunachal Pradesh.[16]

Competition over Resources and Opportunities

The relatively higher literacy rate of the Chakmas and their skillfulness in agriculture also created threat and resentment among the native people of Arunachal Pradesh. According to the *Basic Statistics of North-Eastern Region* of 2000, literacy rate of the native Arunachalis is 41.59 percent while it is approximately 55 percent among the Chakmas as per the opinion of the Chakma respondents provided in 2006.[17] According to the 2011 Census Report of India, the literacy rate among the Arunachalis stood at 66.95 percent.[18] The latest literacy rate of the Chakmas could not be known as the Census on the Chakmas of Arunachal Pradesh was not conducted. However, depending on these

---

16 For details see, "An interview with the AAPSU President, Takom Sanjoy", *Eastern Panorama,* Shillong, October, 1994, 1-3.

17 North Eastern Council (NEC), *Basic Statistics of North-Eastern Region 2000,* (North-Eastern Council, Shillong, 2000), p. 126.

18 For details see, Census of India: Provisional Population Tables - Census 2011, *censusindia.gov.in.* pp. 3-10.

estimates and considering the increasing trend of literacy rate among the Chakmas, it may be argued that the Chakmas are likely to emerge as serious contenders on the opportunity front like employment which is one of the main reasons behind the fear of Chakmas among the native Arunachalis.[19] In Table 2.3, the literacy rate in Arunachal Pradesh in 1991 and in 2000 has been shown along with different States of North East India.

Table 2.4 Literacy rate (in percent) in Arunachal Pradesh and other State of North East India in 1991 and in 2000

State	% of literacy in 1991	% of literacy in 2000
Arunachal Pradesh	41.6	41.59
Assam	52.9	52.89
Manipur	59.9	59.89
Meghalaya	49.1	49.10
Mizoram	82.3	82.27
Nagaland	61.3	61.65
Tripura	60.4	60.44
All India	**52.2**	**52.21**

Source: Compiled from *1991 Census Hand Book* (Registrar General & Census Commissioner, New Delhi, 1996.), p. 3; *Basic Statistics of North-Eastern Region 2000* (North-Eastern Council, Shillong, 2000), p. 126.

According to the information provided by the respondents, the Chakmas grow rice and wheat in the fertile low-lying areas of Miao sub-division and maize, vegetables and horticultural products in the uplands. They are also major suppliers of agricultural produce to Miao and other towns in Changlang district. The Chakmas have shown their high enterprising quality in the field of

19 Susmita Sen Gupta, "Ethnic Issues and All Arunachal Students' Union", *Proceedings of the North East India Political Science Association,* Seventh Annual Conference, (North-Eastern Hill University, Tura Campus, December, 1997), p. 45.

agriculture. Resentment of the locals against the prosperous Chakmas was articulated by the students when the Changlang district unit of the AAPSU enforced an 'economic blockade' upon the Chakmas calling upon the natives not to buy anything from the Chakma refugees. Such a step taken by the AAPSU had a negative fall-out on the economy of the State and the most visible consequence was a shortage of fresh vegetables in the market.[20]

The Inner Line Regulation Act 1873

The Inner Line Regulation Act of 1873 played an important role in determining the AAPSU movement against the Chakmas. The AAPSU often invokes the Legislation passed in 1873 as a source of legal shield for its territorial integrity and exclusiveness forbidden for outsiders to enter and settle in the area. Therefore, the settlement of the Chakmas in Arunachal Pradesh by the Centre is in violation of the Act.[21] In defending this Act, the AAPSU argued that even as the Indian citizens are required to take permission to enter Arunachal Pradesh, the resettlement of the Chakmas in Arunachal Pradesh by the Central government cannot be accepted. On the other side, the Chakmas argued that this Act was made for a different strategic reason of national security and therefore, the same should apply to them.[22] The British government enacted this law not for the welfare of the native people but to create a buffer zone.

---

20 *Ibid.*, p. 45.

21 For details see, "Chakma issue in Arunachal Assembly, Government reiterates demand for immediate deportation", *The Sentinel,* September 26, 1993.

22 Chittagong Hill Tracts Commission, *Life is Not Ours: Land and Human Rights in the Chittagong Hill Tracts, Bangladesh,'* (Copenhagen, Amsterdam: International Work Group for Indigenous Affairs (IWGIA), Organizing Committee Chittagong Hill Tracts Campaign, May 1991), 9.

Table 2.5 Factors responsible for AAPSU Movement against the Chakmas

Sl. No.	Reasons	Percentage of Respondents
1.	Demographic and Political Threats	29
2.	Fear of Land Alienation	11
3.	Pessimism over Chakma issue	10
4.	Competition over Resources	10
5.	All of the above	30
6.	Any other: rapid expansion of education in Arunachal Pradesh, social obligation of the AAPSU, and feeling of exclusiveness with the Inner Line Regulation of 1873 played significant role behind the AAPSU movement against the Chakmas.	10

Table 2.5 shows that 29 percent of the respondents expressed the view that it was the demographic and political threats posed by the Chakmas which led to the AAPSU agitation against the Chakmas. 11 percent of the respondents said that the fear of land alienation was the cause for the AAPSU movement. 10 percent of the respondents were of the view that the pessimism of the Chakma issue led to the AAPSU movement. Yet another 10 percent of the respondents expressed the view that it was due to the fear of competition over resources which influenced the AAPSU to launch its movement against the Chakmas. However, 30 percent of the respondents were of the opinion that all the three above factors were responsible for the AAPSU movement against the Chakmas triggered. The remaining 10 percent of the respondents specified that the rapid expansion of education in Arunachal Pradesh, social obligation of the AAPSU, and feeling of exclusiveness with the Inner Line Regulation of 1873 played significant role behind the AAPSU movement against the Chakmas.

Thus, the opinions expressed by the cross-section of the Chakmas in Arunachal Pradesh clearly show that the AAPSU movement against the Chakmas was generated not by a single factor but the combination of several factors as shown in Table 2.5.

Action Programmes of the AAPSU

Having influenced by the factors discussed, the AAPSU resorted to a series of action programmes which have affected the economic, social and political life of Arunachal Pradesh from time to time. These action programmes have been examined here by dividing them into three phases: 1) Agitation phase fr om 1985 to1990; 2) Insurrection phase from 1990 to 1995; and 3) Civil Disobedience phase from 2004 onwards.

Agitation phase from 1985 to1990

This phase of the AAPSU is characterized by adoption of resolutions and submission of memoranda, ultimatum to the State and Central governments demanding immediate removal of the Chakmas. For example, on August 26, 1985, the AAPSU for the first time adopted a detailed resolution on the Chakma refugee issue in Arunachal Pradesh and submitted a memorandum to the Government of Arunachal Pradesh demanding immediate withdrawal of the refugees on the following grounds:

> The refugees like Chakmas, Tibetans settled permanently in Arunachal Pradesh should be withdrawn immediately from Arunachal Pradesh. It is a sensitive area and as such it restricts entrance of even Indian citizens to Arunachal Pradesh without valid Inner Line permit in accordance with the "Bengal Eastern Frontier Regulation Act of 1873." The meeting feels that the settlement of foreigners

> in Arunachal Pradesh for a prolonged period may be risky to security and hamper the integrity of the territory in due course. Further the concentration of refugees and steady growth of their population has threatened the demographic picture of the area. The government was seized with this problem and the present Honorable Chief Minister said in his broadcast to the people of Arunachal Pradesh on 23rd April, 1980, that the Government of Arunachal Pradesh has taken up the dispersal of these refugees with the Central Government. The meeting now resolves to urge the Government for immediate dispersal of Tibetan and Chakma refugees from Arunachal Pradesh, before they can destroy the demographic harmony of the territory.[23]

Although the Government was quick in its reaction to the memorandum, it explained the intricacies of the problem and also the steps already taken by the government on the issue. Being not satisfied with the clarification and actions taken by the Government, the AAPSU decided to further intensify the agitation by chalking out a year-long programme followed by the submission of an ultimatum to the Government on August 1, 1986, demanding, *inter alia*, the resolution of the Chakma issue within the month of September, 1986, failing which it would go on for more intense agitation. This way the confrontation between the Government and the AAPSU intensified. Further, on August 15, 1986, the AAPSU organized a poster campaign, followed by State *bandh*, a series of district-wise *bandhs* from October 7 to 25, 1986, a hunger strike on November

23 S. Dutta, 'Chakma-Hajong Refugee Problem in Arunachal Pradesh: A Historical Background,' *Proceedings of the North East History Association* (Department of History, North-Eastern Hill University, Shillong), No. 16. (1995), p. 333.

5, 1986, and a *march* to the Legislative Assembly in the same month.[24]

Insurrection phase from 1990 to 1995

The period of AAPSU movement from 1990 to 1995 is marked as the Insurrection phase. During this period the movement was characterized by extremism. *"Chakma dogs go back," "Foreigners quit Arunachal Pradesh or face consequences," "Refugees go back"* – are some of the agitation slogans used by the AAPSU against the Chakmas during the insurrection phase between 1990 and 1995. These slogans not only show the manner in which the AAPSU has responded to the Chakma issue during this phase but also suggest that the issue has been catalyst for change in student politics and movement in Arunachal Pradesh.[25] In May 1994, the AAPSU organized a "Delhi Chalo Movement" (Delhi March) with a delegation of about 400 students. The delegation staged rallies in Delhi for a month to attract the attention of the Central leaders and the Prime Minister. As per newspaper reports, the then Prime Minister, P. V. Narasimha Rao refused to meet the delegation while he agreed to meet the Chakma Student delegation.[26]

The AAPSU movement against the Chakmas reached a flash point when on August 1, 1994 the AAPSU issued "Quit Arunachal' notice to the Chakmas to leave the State peacefully by September 30, 1994. As a follow-up of the notice, the AAPSU organized rallies in different

---

24 For details see, Ultimatum submitted by the AAPSU to the Government of Arunachal Pradesh, August 1, 1986.

25 For details see, Ruben Banerjee, "Chakmas Living Under Notice of Death," *India Today,* New Delhi, October 15, 1994, pp. 42-3.

26 For details see, "Refugee problem takes ugly turn," *The Statesman*, New Delhi, October 3, 1994.

parts of the State including Kokila and Miao, where Chakmas are concentrated.[27] Faced with "Quit Arunachal" notice, the Chakma and Hajong leaders appealed to the Assam Government to provide them shelter in eventuality of attacks by the AAPSU activists. To that effect, the Assam Chief Minister, Hiteswar Saikia had urged his Arunachal counterpart, the then Chief Minister, Gegong Apang, not to push the Chakmas to Assam.[28] Since the Chakmas did not want to quit Arunachal Pradesh despite the 'Quit Arunachal' notice, the AAPSU resorted to violent attacks over the Chakmas. The violent attacks by the AAPSU activists forced over 2000 Chakmas to flee Arunachal Pradesh and take shelter in Sonitpur District of Assam by the end of September, 1994.[29] It was reported that the AAPSU also imposed economic blockade in the Chakma and Hajong inhabited areas and directed the shopkeepers not to sell any commodity even medicines to the Chakmas and Hajongs. Consequently, starvation and disease like malaria engulfed the Chakma villages leading to the deaths of 180 Chakmas and Hajongs. Although the State Government claimed that a medical team was sent to deal with the situation but not a single doctor visited the Chakma inhabited areas.[30]

The Chakma leaders appealed to the national and international human rights organizations such as the Amnesty International (AI) and the Humanity Protection Forum (HPF) for their immediate protection. On

27 For details see, "Amnesty urges Rao to protect Chakmas," *The Statesman,* New Delhi, October 10, 1994.

28 For details see, "Chakmas plea to Assam," *The Telegraph,* Kolkata, October 1, 1994.

29 Committee for Citizenship Rights of the Chakmas of Arunachal Pradesh (CCRCAP), *An Appeal,* New Delhi, August 8, 1995, p. 2.

30 *Ibid.,* p. 2.

September 28, 1994, the Amnesty International expressed concern over the situation and thereafter urged the Prime Minister, P. V. Narasimha Rao to take steps to ensure the safety of the Chakmas. The Amnesty International further alleged that the Chief Minister, Gegong Apang, had not taken any effective steps to control the grave situation. On September 27, 1994, the General Secretary of the Peoples' Rights Organization, Aurobindo Ghosh appealed to the Prime Minister of India, P. V. Narasimha Rao for immediate protection of the Chakmas in Arunachal Pradesh.[31] On September 28, 1994, the Chairman of the Humanity Protection Forum (HPF), Bhagya Chandra Chakma in two separate letters to the Prime Minister, P. V. Narasimha Rao and the Home Minister, S. B. Chavan, requested for immediate protection of the Chakmas of Arunachal Pradesh. The HPF alleged that the Government of Arunachal Pradesh was directly linked to the atrocities perpetrated by the AAPSU on the innocent Chakmas by referring to the instance that the police officials did not take any actions when the AAPSU activists burned down the Chakma houses in front of them.

On September 30, 1994, the Delhi Chakma Students' Union (DCSU) staged a *'dharna'* to protest the alleged atrocities on the Chakmas in Arunachal Pradesh. In the *'dharna,'* the DCSU made slogans like *"Stop burning the Chakma houses," "We want Justice," "We want immediate solution of the Chakma issue," "Give citizenship to the Chakmas"* and so on. This shows that Chakmas did not remain passive over the AAPSU atrocities on them. In a statement during the *'dharna'*, the DCSU said that more 200 houses of the Chakmas were burnt between October 28 and 30, 1994, in the Districts of Papumpare

31 "Protection of Chakmas sought," *The Times of India,* New Delhi, September 28, 1994.

and Changlang followed by other forms of atrocities like torture, discrimination, economic blockade and denial of education to the Chakmas. The DCSU alleged that these atrocities took place under the 'patronage' of the Government of Arunachal Pradesh. Thus, the DCSU appealed to various national and international human rights organizations for protection of the Chakmas in Arunachal Pradesh.[32]

Table 2.6 Reactions of the Chakmas to the AAPSU Movement

Sl. No	Reactions	Percentage of Respondents
1.	Remained passive	20
2.	Organized themselves and built up similar organizations to counter	32
3.	Sought help from the Central Government	18
4.	Sought help from the Courts	20
5.	All of the above	5
6.	Any other: Chakmas organized themselves to resist the atrocities by the AAPSU physically.	5

Table 2.6 shows that 20 percent respondents expressed the view that Chakmas did not remain passive over the AAPSU movement against them. 32 percent respondents said that they organized themselves by forming various organizations such as the All Arunachal Chakma Youths' Federation (AACYF), the Committee for Citizenship Rights of the Chakmas of Arunachal Pradesh (CCRCAP) and students' organizations like the Delhi Chakma Students' Union (DCSU) and maintained connectivity with other students' organizations in India, particularly in the North East. 18 percent respondents said that they also sought help from the Central Government for their security and appealed to the

32 "Chakma students stage dharna," *The Pioneer*, New Delhi, October 1, 1994.

National Human Rights Commission of India for their citizenship rights and they also appealed to various Members of Parliament and the Central Ministers. Another 20 percent respondents said that they were forced to seek justice from the Supreme Court of India and the High Court of Delhi. Five percent respondents said that the Chakmas reacted over the AAPSU movement through all of the above means. However, another 5 percent said that they organized themselves to resist the atrocities by the AAPSU physically.

During this phase the AAPSU also launched "Quit Certificate Movement" in response to Centre's unwillingness to deport the Chakmas from Arunachal Pradesh. On January 25, 1995, it staged a mass procession in the State capital complex of Itanagar in order to surrender all educational certificates of the AAPSU members, including the members of its women wing, the Arunachal Women's Justice Forum (AWJF) to the Governor of the State. After surrendering their certificates to the Governor, the AAPSU staged demonstrations opposing the visit of P. V. Narasimha Rao, the Prime Minister of India, who was scheduled to visit Itanagar to address an election campaign meeting in favour of his party candidates. It also called a ten-hour bandh on the day the Prime Minister, P. V. Narasimha Rao arrived in Itanagar as a reaction to his refusal to meet the AAPSU delegation in Delhi in March 1994.[33] However, the "Quit Certificate Movement" of the AAPSU had not been successful because many of the guardians did not want their boys to surrender their certificates as that might affect their future careers.

---

33 S. Dutta, n. 1, p. 224.

Table 2.7 Politics of AAPSU Movement over the Chakmas issue

Sl. No	Political interests of the AAPSU	Percentage of Respondents
1.	To become political leader in State	12
2.	Ethnic mobilization	23
3.	To influence government decisions	25
4.	To establish student hegemony	20
5.	All of the above	11
6.	Any other: Chakma issue was a potential ground for bringing unity among the different tribes of Arunachal Pradesh.	9

Table 2.7 shows that 12 percent respondents expressed the opinion that the educated elites of Arunachal Pradesh used the platform of the AAPSU as the base for their future career in State politics. They provided examples of those political leaders like Gegong Apang, Jarbom Gamlin, and Takom Sanjay all of whom were either the President or the General Secretary of the AAPSU in the past. 23 percent respondents expressed the view that the AAPSU movement over the Chakma issue was to mobilize ethnic sentiment by projecting the Chakmas as threats to demographic and economic balance in the State. Another 25 percent of the respondents said that the reason behind the AAPSU movement on the Chakma issue was to exert the influence of the educated elites of the State in Government decision-making processes while 20 percent said that it was to establish the hegemony of the elite class through the platform of the AAPSU in the society of Arunachal Pradesh. 11 percent of course said that it was for all of the above. Yet, another 9 percent expressed that the Chakma issue was a potential ground for bringing unity between various students' organizations of different tribal communities of the State such as the

dominant Adi Students' Union. Thus, the AAPSU movement on the Chakma issue was not merely a student movement but an example of politics of student movement for ethnic mobilization by projecting migrant settlers like the Chakmas of Arunachal Pradesh as threats to the demographic and economic balance of the indigenous tribes.

Civil Disobedience phase from 2004 onwards

A third phase or otherwise a new chapter of the AAPSU movement on the Chakma issue began from 2004 when for the first time 1,497 Chakmas have been conferred citizenship rights and were allowed by the Election Commission of India to participate in the Assembly elections held on May 5, 2004, in response to which the AAPSU called for a civil disobedience movement and called upon the people of Arunachal Pradesh to boycott the elections followed by a 48-hour *bandh* all over the State.[34] The conferment of citizenship rights to the Chakmas was related to the background of a petition filed by the Committee for Citizenship Rights of the Chakmas of Arunachal Pradesh (CCRCAP) in the Delhi High Court in 2002 seeking for directions of the Election Commission of India to enroll all the eligible Chakma voters. In a judgment on September 28, 2000, the Delhi High Court directed the Election Commission of India to enroll the eligible Chakmas and Hajongs in the electoral rolls. The Government of Arunachal Pradesh had objected to the judgment of the Delhi High Court and refused to comply with the judgment. In 2002, the CCRCAP filed a contempt petition in the Delhi High Court to uphold the judgment. On March 29, 2003, the

---

34 For details see, Ripunjoy Das, "Chakmas and Hajongs today scripted a new chapter in the electoral history of Arunachal Pradesh," *The Telegraph,* Calcutta, May 6, 2004.

Election Commission of India ordered Special Revision to enroll the Chakma voters pursuant to which about 11,360 eligible Chakma voters claimed for the inclusion of their names in the electorate. Out of these eligible Chakmas, only 1,497 claims were accepted and the rest were rejected at the interference of the Government of Arunachal Pradesh. On June 14, 2003, vide a Cabinet decision the State electoral officials deleted the names of these new Chakma voters from the electoral rolls.[35] Following numerous complaints from the CCRCAP, the Election Commission of India directed the State Government to respect the rule of law and ensure that the Chakma voters who have been once included could not be deleted. But the State Government failed to comply with the directives of the Election Commission after which the Election Commission vide its order dated January 2, 2004, suspended all electoral activities in the four Chakma inhabited Assembly Constituencies such as 14 Doimukh in Papumpare District, 46 Chowkham in Lohit District, 49 Bordumsa-Diyun and 50 Miao in Changlang District until the Chakma voters were included in the electoral rolls.[36]

On February 24, 2004, the AAPSU leaders and the former Chief Minister, Mukut Mithi approached the Gauhati High Court against the Election Commission by a petition seeking quashing of its order of January 2, 2004. The Election Commission vide another order on March 3, 2004, revoked the suspension order but simultaneously ordered the State Election Commission

---

35 For details see, Committee for Citizenship Rights of the Chakmas of Arunachal Pradesh (CCRCAP), *An Appeal,* New Delhi, September 23, 2005, pp.1.

36 For details see, Election Commission of India, *Order*, No. 23/ ARUN/2003, New Delhi, March 3, 2004, pp. 1-3.

of Arunachal Pradesh to include all those 1,497 Chakma voters and publish the electoral rolls forthwith. The AAPSU leaders along with the legislator, T.C. Teli filed another writ petition before the Gauhati High Court seeking stay of the Election Commission's order of March 3, 2004 on the ground that names of Chakma voters cannot be legally included into the Electoral rolls because they did not acquire Inner Line Permits to enter Arunachal Pradesh. No judgment of this case has been declared so far.[37]

On March 23, 2005, the Election Commission of India passed specific Guidelines for investigation and inclusion of all eligible Chakma and Hajong claimants as voters in the electoral rolls of Arunachal Pradesh. In 2009, the AAPSU has filed a Public Interest Litigation (PIL) in Gauhati High Court terming the Election Commission's guidelines to include the names of Chakma refugees in the electoral roll for the Lok Sabha elections as illegal.[38] After that no significant agitation programme of the AAPSU over the Chakma issue has been reported. Viewed in this perspective, the Chakma issue may be considered as an essential component of student politics in Arunachal Pradesh.

---

37 For details see, Committee for Citizenship Rights of the Chakmas of Arunachal Pradesh (CCRCAP), *An Appeal,* New Delhi, August 20, 2004, pp.1-2.

38 For details see, "Students' union files PIL against Chakmas." *The Telegraph, Guwahati,* June 11, 2009.

CHAPTER - III

Chakma Issue and Political Parties of Arunachal Pradesh

There was no antecedent of party politics in Arunachal Pradesh in relation to the Chakma issue until the beginning of the 1980s. Party politics in Arunachal Pradesh began with the first ever Lok Sabha Elections and Legislative Assembly Elections being held in the State in 1977 and 1978 respectively. These elections were contested mainly on development issues. It was only during the second general elections of the State held in 1980 that a political issue like the Chakma issue was adopted for mass mobilization by the political parties of Arunachal Pradesh, particularly the Congress led by Gegong Apang who subsequently came to power on January 18, 1980. On April 23, 1980, the then newly elected Chief Minister of Arunachal Pradesh, Gegong Apang announced through a radio message to the people of Arunachal Pradesh from Dibrugarh station of Assam that his Government has taken up the deportation question of the Chakma and other refugees in Arunachal Pradesh with the Central Government. This marked the beginning of party politics in Arunachal Pradesh in relation to the Chakma issue.[1]

Party Politics and Elections in Arunachal Pradesh

Politics and political socialization in Arunachal Pradesh started with the introduction of Panchayat system way back in 1967.[2] The Agency Council was the apex decision-making body of the Panchayat system. The Agency Council was replaced by Pradesh Council in 1972. Arunachal Pradesh has undergone constitutional changes in its evolution to attain statehood. The then NEFA became a Union Territory on January 20, 1972.[3] It was only in 1975 that the Pradesh Council was declared as a separate Legislative Assembly with 23 members through the 37th Constitutional Amendment Act, 1975 and a Lieutenant Governor was appointed as the head of the Union Territory of Arunachal Pradesh. The first elected Legislative Assembly consisting of 33 members (30 elected members and 3 nominated members) was formed on 4th March 1978, which lasted only for about 20 months. In November 1979, the Assembly was dissolved and President's Rule was imposed which continued till January 1980. The Second General Elections were held in January, 1980. The Third General Elections for Legislative Assembly were held simultaneously with the General Elections for the Eighth Lok

1 For details see, Memorandum No. AAPSU/GS/-7/81-83/56, Pasighat, February 12, 1982 and the Message of Gegong Apang, Chief Minister of Arunachal Pradesh, broadcast from AIR, Dibrugarh, on April 23, 1980.

2 P.S. Dutta, *Economic Development of Arunachal Pradesh A Case Study of North-Eastern Council's Role,* (New Delhi: Vikas Publishing House Pvt. Ltd., 1991), p. 21.

3 For details see, J. N. Choudhury, *Arunachal Pradesh: From Frontier Tracts to Union Territory,* (New Delhi: Cosmo Publications, 1983), pp. 1-10.

Sabha in December, 1984, and the Assembly was constituted in January, 1986. The Union Territory of Arunachal Pradesh became a State with effect from February 20, 1987. The total numbers of seats in the Legislative Assembly were raised to sixty during the General Elections of 1990.[4]

Party politics found its root in Arunachal Pradesh only when the first Lok Sabha and the Legislative Assembly elections were held in 1977 and 1978 respectively. The first regional political party in the State, the Peoples' Party of Arunachal (PPA) was formed in 1977. The Janata party entered the State as early as in 1977. A unit of the Indian National Congress was established in Arunachal Pradesh in 1972. As stated Arunachal Pradesh became a Union Territory in 1972 and was granted a Provisional Legislative Assembly in 1975 in place of the Pradesh Council. On the eve of the Lok Sabha elections of 1977, all the members of the Pradesh Council joined the Indian National Congress en masse under the leadership of P. K. Thungon, the then Chief Minister of Arunachal Pradesh. During the Lok Sabha Elections of 1977, the Congress was the lone political party in Arunachal Pradesh to contest in the two constituencies of the Union Territory namely Arunachal East and Arunachal West. While in the West Constituency, the Congress candidate, Rinchin Khandu Khirme, was declared elected unopposed, the other Constituency was won by an Independent candidate, Bakin Partin.[5] When the Janata party came to power in the Centre in the

---

4 Home: Official Website of the Government of Arunachal Pradesh, India, http://arunachalpradesh,nic.in/, January 1, 2012.

5 A.C. Talukdar, "Regional Political Party in Arunachal Pradesh – Its Nature and Role in State Politics," in B. Pakem (ed.), *Regionalism in India, with Special Reference to North-East India* (New Delhi: Har-Anand Publications, 1993), pp. 290-91.

wake of the Parliamentary Elections of 1977, P. K. Thungon changed his political coat and joined the Janata party with all his followers in March 1977.

Table 3.1 Position of Different Political Parties in Assembly Elections, 1978

Party	Seats Contested	Seats won	Voters polled (in Percent)
Janata Party	29	17	42.08
PPA	20	8	30.24
Congress	1	0	00.45
Independent (32)	NA	5	27.22

Source: Arunachal Pradesh General Elections, Legislative Assembly, 1978, Statistical Report, Chief Election Officer, Arunachal Pradesh, Itanagar.

In February, 1978, the first Legislative Assembly elections of Arunachal Pradesh were held in which the Janata party won majority seats, and on March 4, 1978, the first ministry of Arunachal Pradesh was formed under the leadership of P. K. Thungon. The position of different political parties in the Assembly elections of 1978 has been shown in Table 3.1. But soon P. K. Thungon's Ministry had fallen prey to defections succeeded by the Tomo Riba's Ministry of the PPA which accommodated certain defectors from the Janata party leading to P. K. Thungon's resignation. The change-over was not very smooth. After P. K. Thungon resigned, Gegong Apang, who was a Minister in the Ministry of P. K. Thungon claimed himself as the leader of a newly formed political party called the Arunachal People's Conference (APC) and submitted a list of 22 MLAs claiming them to belong to the Arunachal People's Conference, and staked his claim to form a new government. But within 24 hours of the formation of the APC, many of them defected to PPA.

Table 3.2 Position of Different Political Parties in the Assembly Elections of 1980

Party	Seats Contested	Seats won	Candidates polling nearest votes	Percentage of votes
Congress (I)	28	13	10	42.58
Congress (U)	11	00	02	04.89
PPA	28	17	04	40.98
Independent (2)	17	04	04	11.54

Source: Election Commission of India, *General Election, 1980 to the Legislative Assembly of Arunachal Pradesh*, New Delhi, p. 5.

As a result of frequent defection from one party to another, the first elected Assembly of Arunachal Pradesh was dissolved within 20 months and President's Rule was imposed in November, 1979. Just ahead of the 1980 elections, Gegong Apang along with his former Janata colleagues joined the Congress and came to power in January the same year.[6] The position of different political parties during the Assembly elections of 1980 has been shown in Table 3.2 and position of the 1980 Lok Sabha elections has been shown in Table 3.3.

Table 3.3 Position of Different Political Parties in Lok Sabha Elections, 1980

Party	Seats Contested	Seats won	Percentage of valid Voters polled
Congress (I)	2	2	44.13
Congress (U)	2	0	10.87
PPA	2	0	40.22
Independent	2	0	04.78

Source: Election Commission of India, *Statistical Report on General Elections, 1980, to the 7th Lok Sabha*, Vol. I, New Delhi, 1981, p. 10.

6 *Ibid.*, p. 291.

In the wake of the Lok Sabha Elections of 1977, the newly elected Independent Member of Parliament, Bakin Pertin convened an all Leaders Conference at Pasighat in April, 1977. The Conference was attended by leaders from all over Arunachal Pradesh including the then Minister of Agriculture in the P. K. Thungan Ministry, Tomo Riba. The Conference decided to form a regional political party called the Peoples' Party of Arunachal (PPA) with 'mithun' as its electoral symbol. Bakin Partin was elected as the President and Wanglat Lowangcha, a student leader was elected as the General Secretary. Tomo Riba resigned from the Ministry of P. K. Thunganto become its Vice-President.[7] After the formation, the Peoples' Party of Arunachal (PPA) pledged to the people of Arunachal Pradesh that it would 'work ceaselessly for the good of many and for the happiness of many.' The Election Manifestos of the PPA for the 1980 and 1984 elections pledged to "build an egalitarian society" and a "welfare government" drawn from the visions of Mahatma Gandhi and Jawaharlal Nehru.[8]

But the very purpose behind the PPA's formation was to promote tribal interests and welfare of the people of Arunachal Pradesh.[9] Given the regional agenda of the PPA, it pledged to defend the 'regional identity, preservation of traditional culture and identity, modernization of agriculture, solution of boundary dispute with Assam, and resistance to 'alien culture' of refugees as that of the Chakmas.[10] The PPA described itself as a party regional in character and national in outlook. According to the President of the party, Bakin Partin,

7 Bijan Mohanta, Administrative Development of Arunachal Pradesh 1875-1975, (New Delhi: Uppal Publishing House, 1984), p. 186.

8 A.C. Talukdar, n. 5, p. 292.

9 Bijan Mohanta, n. 7, p. 185.

10 *Ibid.*, p. 294.

this character of the party provided for the ideal basis of co-operation between the PPA and national parties in pursuit of a national objective and was highly welcomed by the student community.[11]

Table 3.4 Position of Different Political Parties in Assembly Elections, 1984

Party	Seats Contested	Seats won	Percentage of votes
Congress (I)	30	21	43.07
Janata Party	03	00	00.38
BJP	06	01	07.69
PPA	13	04	36.74
Independent (63)	23	04	42.15

Source: Election Commission of India, *Statistical Report on General Election, 1984 to the Legislative Assembly of Arunachal Pradesh*, New Delhi, p. 5.

During the 1980 elections, as shown in Table 3.2, although PPA's overall performance was even better than Congress, it could not form the Government because four of its legislators defected to Congress immediately after the elections were over. After the formation of the ministry by the Congress under the leadership of Gegong Apang, many other PPA legislators, including its founder General Secretary, Wanglat Lowangcha joined the Congress. In the 1984 elections, the Congress own the majority, while PPA-Bharatiya Janata Party (BJP) alliance failed to return any candidate in the Lok Sabha elections but won only 5 seats in the Assembly elections four for PPA and one for BJP as shown in Table 3.4.

From what has been described, the nature of regional and national political parties in Arunachal Pradesh may be summarized as follows:

---

11 A. C. Talukdar, n. 5, p. 293.

1. Both national and regional political parties in Arunachal Pradesh encouraged politics of defection;
2. There was a general tendency among the leaders and people of the State to support the ruling party in the Centre;
3. Too much intra-party differences;[12] and
4. The regional political party, PPA was of dual character – 'regional at state level and at national level it floats in the mainstream of national life.'[13]

Chakma issue and Political Parties

The party politics in Arunachal Pradesh developed rather through intra-party differences, defection and the influence of national ideology to build an egalitarian society than on socio-political issues like the Chakma issue. Although the PPA pledged for the preservation of traditional culture and identity of the indigenous tribes of Arunachal Pradesh and resistance to alien culture, party politics in Arunachal Pradesh was mostly concerned about development issues.[14] However, in the Brahmaputra Valley of Assam, party politics with 'foreign national' issue had already taken roots in the 1980s which soon influenced the politics of other States in North East India including Arunachal Pradesh.[15] The Congress party in Arunachal Pradesh under the leadership of Gegong Apang did not lose time to engage the Chakma issue for political mobilization in the State. However, the Chakma issue did not become prominent in the party

12 BijanMohanta, n. 7, p. 188.

13 A. C. Talukdar, n. 5, p. 293.

14 BijanMohanta, n. 7, p. 201.

15 *Ibid.*, p. 202.

politics of Arunachal Pradesh until the Centre declared to grant Indian citizenship to the Chakmas in 1992.

The Union Government of India decided to grant citizenship to the Chakmas of Arunachal Pradesh only when two members of Parliament, Kabindra Purkayastha and Lalit Oraon raised the question on the 'grant of Indian citizenship to the Chakma refugees in Arunachal Pradesh,' in the Lok Sabha in 1992. The question was answered in the Lok Sabha on February 27, 1992 by the Union Minister of State.[16] The then Union Minister of State, M.M. Jacob answered to the House that the Chakmas would be granted citizenship on the basis of the Assam Accord of 1985. The Assam Accord provided provisions for grant of citizenship to all those persons who came and settled in India prior to January 1, 1966. The Chakmas had migrated to Arunachal Pradesh in 1964, almost two years before this dateline. On this ground, Chakmas of Arunachal Pradesh were eligible for Indian citizenship.[17] As a reaction to the Union Minister's answer, Laeta Umbrey, a Congress Member of Parliament from Arunachal Pradesh pointed out in the Lok Sabha on October 5, 1992, that as a 'matter of urgent public importance' Chakma settlers needed to be deported immediately from Arunachal Pradesh. In a reply to Laeta Umbrey on September 23, 1992, the Union Minister of State, M. M. Jacob stated that:

> "According to information given by the State Government, present population of the Chakma and Hajong refugees who were settled in Arunachal Pradesh during 60s is around 30,000. These refugees

16 For details see, Lok Sabha, Unstarred question No. 522, February 27, 1992.

17 Rajya Sabha Committee on Petitions, *Hundred and Fifth Report,* (New Delhi: RajyaSabha Secretariat, August 14, 1997), p. 7.

were settled in Arunachal Pradesh in consultation with the State Administration under a definite plan of rehabilitation. No reports have been received regarding involvement of these refugees in anti-national activities. The presence of these refugees in the areas has also not resulted so far in any major law and order problem.... A Central Team which visited Arunachal Pradesh in 1982 to study the problems of these refugees expressed the view that the grant of citizenship would introduce an element of responsible social behaviour in these refugees. Being "new migrants", viz., refugees from Bangladesh who came to India between 1964 and 1971 (March 25, 1971), they are eligible to the grant of citizenship. Further, a very large proportion of these refugees would have been born in India, therefore, would be automatically entitled to the grant of citizenship.

Keeping the above in view, there is no question of deporting these refugees from the State of Arunachal Pradesh. The general public in the State of Arunachal Pradesh will have to be convinced that the burden of rehabilitation of these refugees will have to be shared by the country as a whole including Arunachal Pradesh."[18]

The statement of the Union Minister underscores two important aspects: first, the Chakma issue became politically more significant than ever before with the Centre's declaration of granting citizenship to the Chakmas, and second, the issue has become a potential ground for party politics in Arunachal Pradesh.

On March 4, 1992, the then opposition leader in the Lok Sabha L.K. Advani wrote a letter to the Home

18 Letter D. O. No. 12/16/92/-MZ, Minister of State for Home and Parliamentary Affairs, India, North Block, New Delhi, September 23, 1992.

Minister S.B. Chavan in which he said, "I fail to understand why Chakmas living in Arunachal Pradesh are being treated differently when the Chakmas living in Assam, Tripura and Mizoram have been given recognition as Scheduled Tribes. This is unfair and unjust.... I shall be grateful if you could see that due justice is given to the Chakmas living in Arunachal Pradesh?"[19] On March 31, 1992, Somnath Chatterjee, a member of Parliament wrote a letter to the then Prime Minister of India, P. V. Narasimha Rao, stating that the Chakmas in Arunachal Pradesh are facing serious difficulties in the matter of employment and educational facilities. He earnestly requested the Prime Minister to consider the appeal of the Chakmas sympathetically.[20] On April 8, 1992, the Prime Minister, P. V. Narasimha Rao, replied to Somnath Chatterjee that he had received his letter enclosed with a representation of the Committee for Citizenship Rights of the Chakmas of Arunachal Pradesh. The Prime Minister, P. V. Narasimha Rao, stated in the reply that he had asked the Home Minister to look into the matter.[21]

In September, 1992, the Peoples Rights Organisation (PRO) in Delhi presented a report on "The Question of Indian Citizenship Rights of the Stateless Chakmas and Hajongs of Arunachal Pradesh," to the Government of India and in relation to that the PRO also staged a 'dharna' in Delhi protesting against the alleged atrocities over the Chakmas by the local Singhphos, the Tangsas,

---

19 Letter of L. K. Advani, Leader of opposition, Lok Sabha to the Minister of Home Affairs, S. B. Chavan, New Delhi, dated March 4, 1992.

20 Letter of Somnath Chatterjee, Member of Parliament, to the Prime Minister P. V. Narasimha Rao, New Delhi, dated March 31, 1992.

21 Letter of P. V. Narasimha Rao, Prime Minister of India, Government of India, to Somnath Chatterjee, Member of Parliament, Leader of CPI (M), Lok Sabha, New Delhi April 8, 1992.

the Nishis, the AAPSU, the Arunachal Pradesh Police (APP), and the Government of Arunachal Pradesh.[22]

On December 3, 1992, the Legislative Assembly of Arunachal Pradesh witnessed a furor over Jacob's statement. The former opposition leader from the PPA, Wanglat Lowangcha who joined the Congress after the elections of 1984, called upon the attention of the House by saying, 'the day is not far when Chakmas will become members of our Assembly' and soon their growing population will create problems for tribal identity in the State. The former Congress Minister, Mukut Mithi, blamed the Central government for delaying the deportation of the refugees. The Home Minister, Neelam Taram said that Chakmas are detrimental to the State. Shri Gegong Apang, Chief Minister, said that the East Bengal Frontier Regulation Act 1873 was to be enforced. The Chief Minister further added that a corrigendum must be given by the Union Minister, M.M. Jacob because granting citizenship to the Chakma refugees might lead the youth of the State to taking up arms to check the inflow of Chakmas.[23]

Over the time, Gegong Apang became most influential leader of the Congress in Arunachal Pradesh and managed to rule the State almost uninterruptedly since the State was introduced to electoral politics in 1977 and 1978. In the Assembly debate of December 3, 1992, Gegong Apang argued that the State Government in particular and people in general could not reconcile with the frequent pressure from the Centre to absorb the

22 Peoples' Rights Organization (PRO), *The Question of Indian Citizenship Rights of the Stateless Chakmas and Hajongs of Arunachal Pradesh*, (New Delhi, September, 1992), p. 15

23 Kumar Bhakti, "Strong resentment over Jacob's statement, Chakmas are citizens of Arunachal," *The Echo of Arunachal*, December 9-15, 1992.

Chakmas in the local milieu. The people here have been urging the Centre to send back those refugees and are apprehensive of demographic imbalances and serious socio-political implications. The Congress government in the State has adopted a few resolutions during the last decade, urging the Centre to deport these refugees either to their native land in Bangladesh or to any other part of the country. A delegation led by him submitted a memorandum to the Centre, highlighting the various implications of this problem. The Centre was, however silent and non-committal on the subject, since it was also in a dilemma, as no other state would accept them. The refugee issue was frequently raised in the State Assembly and several resolutions were already adopted demanding the deportation of these refugees from the State. Our party is under tremendous pressure from all sides and is compelled to move resolutions by voice votes. The party had already registered objections to the Central team which visited the State earlier in 1982.[24]

Given the anti-Chakma sentiment already flourished by the AAPSU movement as examined in the second chapter, the centrality of the Chakma issue as political capital further intensified in the party politics of Arunachal Pradesh before the Elections to be held in 1995. Since the 1980 Assembly elections, Gegong Apang had been using the AAPSU platform as support basc for mass mobilization.[25] As discussed in the Second Chapter, on the eve of the elections to be held on March 11, 1995, P.V. Narasimha Rao, the Prime Minister of India was scheduled to visit the capital to address a

24 For details see, "Chakma issue in Arunachal Assembly, Government reiterates demand for immediate repatriation," *The Sentinel,* September 26, 1993.

25 Sanjoy Hajarika, "The Chakmas' flight to nowhere," *The Indian Express,* New Delhi, October 17, 1994.

campaign meeting in favour of his party candidates. On January 25, 1995, the AAPSU launched "Quit Certificate Movement" against indecisive stand of the Central Government on the deportation of the Chakmas. The AAPSU opposed the visit of the Prime Minister and called a ten-hour bandh in the State. The reason for calling the bandh was that the Prime Minister, P.V. Narasimha Rao refused to meet the AAPSU delegation during their 'Delhi Chalo Movement' (Delhi March) in 1994. When asked about that, the Prime Minister said he was not informed about the AAPSU delegation.[26] However, the Prime Minister assured from his personal level to find an amicable solution to the Chakma issue soon.

During the 1995 elections, the election manifesto of the Congress was mainly centered around the Chakma issue and the boundary dispute with Assam which were focused even during the Prime Minister's campaign programmes. The other contesting parties, the Janata Dal (JD), the Janata Party (JP), the Bharatiya Janata Party (BJP), and the Independents all pledged to the people to resolve the Chakma issue once they come to power. The main regional party of the State, the PPA, joined the Janata Dal in 1989. The peoples' verdict again came in favour of the Congress and Gegong Apang having elected with absolute majority with 43 seats in the 60 member Assembly. The Independents won 4, the Janata Dalwon 3, and the Janata Partygot 2, while the BJP returned with nil. In Table 3.5, the position of different contesting political parties in the 1995 Assembly elections has been shown.

---

26 For details see, S. Dutta, 'Student Movement in Arunachal Pradesh,' in A. K. Baruah (ed.), *Student Power in North-East India Understanding Student Movements,* (New Delhi: Regency Publications, 2002), p. 224.

Table 3.5 Position of Different Political Parties in Assembly Elections, 1995

Party	Seats Contested	Seats won	Percentage of votes
Congress (I)	60	43	50.50
Janata Party	05	02	02.53
BJP	15	00	15.07
Janata Dal	34	03	17.24
Independent (59)	12	04	26.26

Source: Election Commission of India, *Statistical Report on General Election, 1995 to the Legislative Assembly of Arunachal Pradesh*, New Delhi, p. 7.

Considering the serious nature and complexity of the Chakma issue, an All Party Legislative meeting was held on September 6, 1995, under the Chairmanship of Honorable Chief Minister, Geong Apang, in which it was decided to organize a Peoples' Referendum Rally in Rajiv Gandhi Stadium at Naharlagun on September 20, 1995 demanding immediate deportation of the Chakma and Hajong refugees from the State. After the rally, a-six point resolution was passed on the demand of deportation of refugees.[27] In the Rally Chief, Minister, Gegong Apang and his party members said that they would resign from the primary membership of the Congress if the Centre did not take measures over their appeal to deport the Chakmas from Arunachal Pradesh.

Again on December 21, 1995, the debate on Chakma issue took place in the Second Legislative Assembly of Arunachal Pradesh. The Janata Dal legislator, T.C. Telimade an intervention on the Chakma issue demanding ratification of the resolution taken on September 20, 1995 vis-à-vis the Chakma issue. He

27 Organising Committee Peoples' Referendum Rally, *An Appeal*, Naharlagun, Arunachal Pradesh, September 20, 1995.

reiterated his persuasion with the Central leaders in Delhi like S.R. Bomai, V.P. Singh and Rambilas Paswan to do something on the Chakma issue. The Janata Party had the same stand.[28] To keep some clarification on records, the Chief Minister, Gegong Apang rose and said that all the parties, 60 members of the Assembly and the people of Arunachal Pradesh are inseparable on the Chakma issue. But he requested all the members of the Assembly to wait until the Supreme Court judgment to be given on the Chakma issue soon and explained the provision in rule 123 of the Procedure and Conduct of Arunachal Pradesh Legislative Assembly that it was not permissible to take further resolution on an issue pending in the Supreme Court.[29]

Chakma issue and Formation of Arunachal Congress

The Arunachal Congress (AC) was formed in September 1996 by the then Chief Minister, Gegong Apang and is said to be the direct outcome of the Peoples' Referendum Rally of September 20, 1995 which was organized for demanding immediate deportation of the Chakma and Hajong refugees from Arunachal Pradesh. At his first press conference after the swearing-in ceremony, Gegong Apang said his new party's policy would be to deport the Chakma and Hajong refugees from the state without creating a human problem. The indigenous people of Arunachal Pradesh had high expectations on him and the party. As stated earlier, the Chief Minister, Gegong Apang, declared in the Peoples' Referendum Rally on September 20, 1995, at Naharlagun, that he and his party members would resign

28 Official Report, *Proceedings of the Arunachal Pradesh Second Legislative Assembly,* Third Session, Assembly Secretariat, Arunachal Pradesh, Naharlagu, December 21-22, 1995, p. 59.

29 *Ibid.,* p. 77.

from the primary membership of their party if the demand for the deportation of the Chakmas was not accepted by Delhi.[30] The Rally was organized with the initiative Gegong Apang himself because he was losing popular support for not being able to bring a solution to the Chakma issue.

The creation of the Arunachal Congress is also a direct result of Prime Minister, P.V. Narasimha Rao's failure to resolve the Chakma issue. As stated, during his visit to the State capital of Itanagar in 1995 to campaign for his party candidates, the Prime Minister, P.V. Narasimha Rao committed to find an amicable solution to the Chakma issue. But nothing happened over a year or so, Gegong Apang revolted against P.V. Narasimha Rao, and then along with his Cabinet colleagues resigned *en masse* from the Congress party and thereafter formed regional party called Arunachal Congress. Gegong Apang took with him 54 legislators out of total 60 in the Arunachal Assembly to his new party. In the Lok Sabha elections of 1998, the Arunachal Congress won both the seats of Arunachal Pradesh. The party made an alliance with the Bharatiya Janata Party (BJP) and became a founding member of the National Democratic Alliance (NDA). Gegong Apang's son, Omak Apang who had been elected from the constituency of Arunachal West, was later made a Central Minister in the NDA Government in Delhi.[31]

However, the Arunachal Congress did not last long. Soon after the 1998 elections there was an intra-party squabble. Wangcha Rajkumar, who had been elected to

---

30 Subir Ghosh, *Frontiers Travails – Northeast: The Politics of a Mess*, (New Delhi: Macmillan India Ltd., 2001), pp.116-7.

31 Lima Sasai Aier, (ed.), *Encyclopaedia of Arunachal Pradesh*, Vol. 1 & 2, (New Delhi: Anmol Publications Pvt. Ltd., 2009), pp. 12-13.

the Lok Sabha twice from the Arunachal East Constituency in 1996 and in 1998, alleged that Gegong Apang had resorted to nepotism when his son Omak Apang was made a Central Minister in place of him. As a result, Gegong Apang expelled Wangcha Rajkumar and five other State Ministers who had sided with him. One of the ex-ministers, Mukut Mithi also split from the Congress and formed the Arunachal Congress (Mukut Mithi). The Arunachal Congress of Mukut Mithi was able to gather 40 members of the State Legislative Assembly which eventually led him to form the Government. Initially, both the Arunachal Congress of Gegong Apang and Arunachal Congress of Mukut Mithi supported the Atal Bihari Vajpayee's NDA Government in the Centre. As Wangcha Rajkumar was not allotted any ministerial posts in the NDA Government, Mukut Mithi and his Arunachal Congress merged with the Indian National Congress ahead of the 1999 Assembly elections.[32]

On the eve of the mid-term Lok Sabha elections of 1999, Gegong Apang and his Arunachal Congress made an alliance with the BJP. The Arunachal Congress-BJP alliance lost in both Parliamentary Constituencies of Arunachal Pradesh to Indian National Congress (INC) in the mid-term Parliamentary elections of 1999. Gegong Apang's son Omak Apang lost from Arunachal West Parliamentary Constituency to the Indian National Congress candidate, Jarbom Gamlin who scored 131483 votes (55.87 percent) out of the 2,35,319 total voters in the Constituency while in the Arunachal East Parliamentary Constituency, the BJP candidate, Tapir Gao lost to the INA candidate Wangcha Rajkumar, who scored 110792 votes (58.21 percent) out of the 1,90,344 total voters in the Constituency.

32 *Ibid.*, p. 13.

In the Legislative Assembly Elections of 1999, except Gegong Apang, no other candidate was elected from the Arunachal Congress of Gegong Apang and the BJP. About 38 candidates from the Arunachal Congress contested in these elections. The reasons behind the gross defeat of Arunachal Congress-BJP alliance included Gegong Apang's failure to resolve the Chakma issue and the threat from the National Socialist Council of Nagaland of Isak and Muivah group (NSCN-IM) in the area not to vote for them.[33]

On the eve of the Lok Sabha elections 2004, another split had taken place in the Indian National Congress (INC) in Arunachal Pradesh. The then President of the INC unit in the State, Kameng Dolo left the INC on July 25, 2003, and thereafter formed another party called the Congress (Kameng Dolo). With the split in the INC and the formation of the Congress (Kameng Dolo), Gegong Apang formed a front called United Democratic Front consisting of himself, Congress (Kameng Dolo), the expelled Congress legislators and two Independents. In total, Gegong Apang was able to gather 41 Legislators with him. On August 3, 2003, Gegong Apang formed the Government and was sworn in as the Chief Minister of the State. On August 30, 2003, Gegong Apang joined the BJP along with 41 Members of the Legislative Assembly. On Gegong Apang's joining the BJP, Arunachal Pradesh became the first BJP ruled State Government in the North East.[34]

The Arunachal Congress earlier formed by Gegong Apang did, however, continue to exist as a party even after its founder, Gegong Apang had joined the BJP. On the eve of the 2004 Lok Sabha Elections, the Arunachal

33 *Ibid.*, p. 13.

34 Sushanta Talukdar, "Assembly Elections, A Volte-face in Arunachal" *Frontline*, Vol. 21, No. 19, New Delhi, September 11-24, 2004.

Congress called for a boycott of the elections as a protest against the enrollment of Chakma and Hajong refugees as voters in the electoral rolls. Finally, the Arunachal Congress decided to contest the Lok Sabha elections of 2004 in alliance with Indian National Congress. However, The Arunachal Congress-INC alliance lost in both the Parliamentary Constituencies of Arunachal Pradesh.[35]

Chakma issue and Political Parties after 2009

In 2009 Assembly Elections, the Congress came to power in Arunachal Pradesh by a two-third majority. Dorjee Khandu became the new Chief Minister of Arunachal Pradesh. The Election Manifestos of the Congress and other political parties in the 2009 Assembly Elections pledged for development, security and peace in Arunachal Pradesh. The Chakma issue was not included in these manifestoes like before. However, on August 12, 2010, Chief Minister Dorjee Khandu wrote to the Election Commission of India requesting it to reinvestigate the inclusion of Chakmas and Hajongs as voters in the electoral rolls. He also constituted a nine-member high-level committee under the Chairmanship of a representative of the Union Home Ministry in June 2010 to study the Chakma and Hajong settlement report.[36]

In 2019 general elections in Arunachal Pradesh, the BJP candidates, Kiren Rijiju (West) and Tapir Gao (East) won with huge margin defeating the INC candidates, Nabam Tuki (West) and Lowangcha Wanglet (East). The INC candidates lost mainly because they failed to solve the Chakma issue earlier when they were in power and BJP candidates won because they have given new

35 *Ibid.*, p. 13.

36 "Khandu moves poll panel after violence," *The Telegraph*, Guwahati, Ausust 12, 2010.

promise to relocate the Chakma and Hajong refugees from the state.

Following the Lok Sabha elections, the BJP and its allies had a landslide victory in legislative elections too winning 41 seats out of the total 60 and Pema Khandu took oath as Arunachal Pradesh Chief Minister on 29 May 2019.

On August 26, 2021, Chief Minister Pema Khandu and Union Law and Justice Minister Kiren Rijiju announced that the Chakma-Hajong refugees will be relocated from the state which has again elicited an extreme response from the indigenous tribal population of the state and its settlers. The Chakma and Hajong communities in Arunachal said that they outright reject the idea. Further, they demanded that the long-standing refugee issue be fully and permanently resolved at the earliest by providing full rights to them as Indian citizens in Arunachal. On the other hand, tribal groups, including apex student body AAPSU and several political parties have welcomed the announcement to shift Chakma-Hajong settlers out of the state.[37]

Table 3.6 Role of Political Parties in relation to the Chakma issue

Sl. No	Role of Political Parties	%age of Respondents
1.	Speak in favor of the Chakma people	Nil
2.	Use the Chakma issue for political mobilization	26
3.	Keep the Chakma issue alive for political interest	24
4.	Raise the Chakma issue only around elections	30
5.	All of the above except number 1	7
6.	Any other: political parties played double standards over the Chakma problem	13

37 "Proper plan needed for Ckakma-Hajong relocation", *The Arunachal Times*, Itanagar, August 26, 2021.

According to Table 3.6, No respondents expressed that political parties spoke in favor of the Chakmas. 26 percent of the respondents said that political parties rather used the Chakma issue for political mobilization pledging that they would resolve the issue once they come to power. 24 percent expressed that the political parties kept the issue alive to make political benefit out of the Chakma issue while 30 percent said that political parties raised the issue only during the elections. Seven percent of the respondents agreed with all of the above views. However, another 13 percent of the respondents said that political parties played double standards over the Chakma problem, for example, when they failed to resolve the issue, they put the blame on the Centre.

Going by the development of party politics in the state as discussed in this chapter, it is clear that the Chakma citizenship issue not only brought changes in the nature of party politics in Arunachal Pradesh but also led to the creation of a regional political party in the State namely the Arunachal Congress (AC). Prior to the Chakma issue, the party politics of the state evolved with 'development' issue which led to the formation of the first regional political party, the Peoples' Party of Arunachal (PPA) in 1977.

CHAPTER IV

Centre-State Conflict and the Chakma Issue

Although the Chakma refugees were settled in Arunachal Pradesh way back in 1964, the question of their citizenship rights was left undecided by the Government of India for nearly three decades. As discussed in the foregoing chapter that the Union Government of India decided to grant citizenship to the Chakmas of Arunachal Pradesh only in 1992 which greatly affected party politics of Arunachal Pradesh. However, the decision of the Centre to grant citizenship to the Chakmas has also been a cause of conflict between the Union Government and the Government of Arunachal Pradesh. The beginning of the conflict has been evident from the heated debate the Legislative Assembly of Arunachal Pradesh had on December 3, 1992 in which the Chief Minister, Gegong Apang said that the decision of the Centre to grant citizenship to the Chakmas was not acceptable on the part of his Government.[1]

1 For details see, Kumar Bhakti, "Strong resentment over Jacob's statement, Chakmas are citizens of Arunachal," *The Echo of Arunachal,* Itanagar, December 9-15, 1992.

Having observed the development in Delhi, the Government of Arunachal Pradesh reiterated its demand for immediate deportation of Chakma and other refugees residing in different parts of the State. The State Assembly on September 24, 1993, expressed grave concern over the Centre's passive attitude towards the burning refugee problem. The House unanimously condemned the 'dharna' organized by the PRO in Delhi and considered the action as unconstitutional. Clarifying the Government stand on the issue, the Chief Minister Gegong Apang said that people of this 'virgin paradise' were raising their voices demanding the deportation of refugees since NEFA days through various resolutions adopted by the Assembly, students' organization, and political forum. It was unfortunate that the Centre paid no attention, Apang lamented. Moreover, repeated deputations to the succeeding Central Governments, Home Ministers, Prime Ministers, and Presidents of India have failed to yield any result so far. While terming the statement of M. M. Jacob on granting citizenship to the Chakmas, Gegong Apang expressed concern that instead of voicing against the issue, the Centre instigated the Chakmas to move to the Supreme Court. Gegong Apang's leadership rejected the Centre's directives on the issue earlier and continued to do so to safeguard the interest of the peace-loving innocent people of the State.[2]

From August 20 to 22, 1994, the Committee for Citizenship Rights of the Chakmas of Arunachal Pradesh (CCRCAP) organized a three-day hunger strike as a mark of protest against the Government of India's half-hearted approach and Arunachal Government's opposition to the implementation of the policy decision taken by the Union

2 For details see, "Chakma issue in Arunachal Assembly, Government reiterates demand for immediate deportation," *The Sentinel*, Guwahati, September 26, 1993.

Government to grant citizenship rights to the Chakmas and Hajongs in Arunachal Pradesh. The CCRCAP questioned the Union Government as to why it is silent when all the constitutional rights of the Chakmas were being taken away? The State Government had already banned employment rights to the Chakmas through an official circular issued on September 29, 1980 and also banned issuance of ration cards to the Chakmas on October 31, 1991. There was no action from the State Government when on February 5, 1983, the AAPSU activists attacked six Chakma villages and burned down their houses to ashes in Balijan Circle of Subansiri District. It was reported that the Arunachal Pradesh Police (APP) has let loose a reign of terror against the Chakmas. The Chakmas and Hajongs are now suspended between the threat of deportation on the one side, and grant of Indian citizenship on the other.[3] Thus, the Committee for Citizenship Rights of the Chakmas of Arunachal Pradesh (CCRCAP) demanded immediate implementation of Government of India's decision to grant citizenship to the Chakmas, restoration of all the *de facto* rights arbitrarily revoked by the State Government and enrolment of all eligible Chakma and Hajong voters in the Electoral Rolls.[4]

On July 7, 1994, the Union Minister of State for Home P. M. Sayeed indicated in a letter to Noydak Yonggam, a Rajya Sabha Member of Parliament from Arunachal that citizenship may be granted to the Chakmas and Hajongs settled in Arunachal Pradesh in 1964. In his letter, Sayeed stated that the Centre had already examined the matter in details and found that

3 Peoples' Rights Organization (PRO), *The Question of Indian Citizenship Rights of the Stateless Chakmas and Hajongs of Arunachal Pradesh*, (New Delhi, September, 1992), p. 15.

4 Committee for Citizenship Rights of the Chakmas of Arunachal Pradesh (CCRCAP), *An Appeal,* New Delhi, August 20-22, 1994.

the Chakmas, Hajongs, and Tibetan refugees had settled in Arunachal in consultation with the then NEFA Administration. The policy of the Union Government was that refugees who came to India before March 25, 1971 would be considered for Indian citizenship. However, on September 9, 1994, the Arunachal Pradesh Legislative Assembly once again adopted a resolution demanding deportation of the refugees from the State in opposition to Sayeed's statement. During the Assembly sessions, the Chief Minister Gegong Apang pointed out that the Centre was behaving not only step-motherly with the people of Arunachal Pradesh but was also provoking the peace-loving people in the State. Similar resolutions were adopted by the House four times since 1977 demanding deportation of 'foreign nationals.' On August 15,1995, the AAPSU gave a 15-hour 'bandh' call with tacit support from the State Government.[5]

However, the Government of Arunachal Pradesh set a deadline on the deportation of the refugees by December 31, 1995. The Chief Minister of Arunachal Pradesh, Gegong Apang told the media in Calcutta on December 8, 1995, that if the Centre fails to take decision on the deportation of the Chakma refugees by the year end of 1995, it may lose Arunachal as all the Congress MLAs in the State are unhappy about the Centre's pro-Chakma stand and so are ready to resign and go for a regional party. It is now up to "Delhi to choose between the Arunachalis and the Chakmas.[6] The Chief Minister said the Centre had settled the Chakma refugees from the erstwhile East Pakistan in 1964 despite opposition from

---

5 For details see, "Refugee problem takes ugly turn," *The Statesman*, New Delhi, October 3, 1994, p.10.

6 For details see, Ashis Chakrabarty, "Arunachal CM sets deadline on refugee deportation," *The Indian Express*, Calcutta, December 8, 1995.

the local people. At that time, Arunachalis had no voice or representation in the administration of the Assam State whose jurisdiction extended to the region.[7] Thus, it has been seen that the Government of Arunachal Pradesh not only launched a propaganda war against the Centre on the Chakma issue but also threatened that the people of Arunachal Pradesh might start an agitation for "right to self-determination."[8]

Views of the Ministry of Home Affairs

When the conflict between the Centre and the State of Arunachal Pradesh became extreme, the Rajya Sabha Committee on Petitions was formed on August 23, 1995 at a sitting in the Rajya Sabha under the Chairmanship of Sangh Priya Gautam on the Petitions signed by Snehadini Talukdar of Mizoram and Subimal Chakma of Delhi pertaining to the problems faced by the Chakmas in Mizoram and Arunachal Pradesh. The Committee submitted its report on August 14, 1997. It has obtained written comments from the Ministry of Home Affairs on the Chakma issue. The Ministry supplied the comments on the basis of its own perception as the State Government did not supply the information asked for on the various issues raised in the petition.[9] The comments of the Ministry of Home Affairs in brief were:

1. About 15,000 Chakmas and Hajongs out of 140,000 refugees, who entered India from erstwhile East Pakistan (now Bangladesh), were settled from 1964 to 1969 in the then NEFA (now Arunachal Pradesh). In addition to a rehabilitation grant, each family was allotted land

---

7 *Ibid.*

8 *Ibid.*

9 Rajya Sabha Committee on Petition, Hundred and Fifth Report, (New Delhi: Rajya Sabha Secretariat, August 14, 1997), pp.2-3.

varying from 5 acres to 10 acres (depending upon the size of the family). A total of Rs. 130.41 lakhs was spent by the Central Government till 1968 when the scheme was transferred to the NEFA Administration for further implementation.[10]

2. The local tribals have resented the presence of the Chakmas due to encroachment by them on lands outside the original settlements. The fact that the Chakmas have developed the original forest land into good agricultural fields has also become a source of envy. It has also been alleged that the Chakmas have been indulging in criminal activities and contributed to the denudation of forests and depletion of wild life. Their present population in Arunachal Pradesh is estimated to be between 45,000 and 65,000.[11]

3. During talks between the Prime Ministers of India and Bangladesh in 1972, it was agreed, inter alia, that Bangladesh would take back the refugees who came to India after 25 March 1971. Under the Citizenship Rules of 1955, applications for registration as Indian citizens are required to be submitted to the Central Government by the Collector of the concerned district through the State Government. However, as regards the Chakmas and Hajongs settled in Arunachal Pradesh, the State Government has raised objection to their continued presence in the State and has demanded either their repatriation to

---

10 Ministry of Home Affairs (North East Division) on the petition pertaining to the problems being faced by the Chakma Tribal Population in Mizoram and Arunachal Pradesh vide their Office Memo No. 13/15/95-NE September 18,1996.

11 *Ibid.*

Bangladesh or their re-settlement in some other part of the country.[12]

4. Following the agitation, during 1994, led by the All Arunachal Pradesh Student's Union (AAPSU), a series of violent incidents targeting the Chakmas were reported. While the Ministry of Home Affairs had advised the State Government of Arunachal Pradesh to ensure protection of life and liberty of all residents including the Chakma and Hajong refugees, the affected persons had filed a complaint with the National Human Rights Commission (NHRC). The Chakmas had, inter-alia, alleged harassment and intimidation and sought some relief from the Commission. The allegations included withdrawal of ration cards and trade licenses and denial of medical, educational and employment facilities. The NHRC had filed a writ petition in the Supreme Court in November 1995. The State Government, in their counter affidavit did not comment specifically on the withdrawal of ration cards and trade licences and denial of employment opportunities. However, it was indicated that the State Government had incurred considerable expenditure on providing health, water supply, education and social welfare facilities in the Chakma inhabited areas. It was contended that health centres and schools were established and maintained by the State Government.[13]

5. The Supreme Court, after a detailed hearing on January 9, 1996 disposed off the matter with the directions, inter-alia, that the State Government

---

12 *Ibid.*

13 *Ibid.*

of Arunachal Pradesh shall ensure that the life and personal liberty of each and every Chakma residing within the State shall be protected and that, except in accordance with law, the Chakmas shall not be evicted from their homes and shall not be denied domestic life and comfort therein. The Supreme Court further directed that the applications made for registration of the Chakmas as citizens of India shall be forwarded by the Collector of the concerned District to the Central Government for its consideration in accordance with the law, which was heard and dismissed by the Supreme Court on August 5,1996. The Central Government has so far not received any applications from the State Government of Arunachal Pradesh.[14]

6. The Central Government, on its part, had constituted a High-Level Group under the chairmanship of the union Home Minister with representatives from both the Central and State Governments with a view to identify the course of action to be adopted for a resolution of the problem. The Group met on January 5, 1996 and constituted an official level Sub-Committee comprising senior officials from both the Central and State Governments for ascertaining the detailed facts and suggesting the course of action which could be adopted fora resolution of the problem. The Ministry of Home Affairs had written to the state Government on February 16, 1996 requesting for convenience of the State Government for a visit by the official level Sub-Committee. The Chief Secretary, Arunachal Pradesh after dismissal of the Review Petition by

14 *Ibid.*

the Supreme Court, agreed to allow a visit to Arunachal Pradesh by the official level Sub-Committee. A programme is being chalked out accordingly.[15]

Views of the Home Secretary on the Chakmas Issue in Arunachal Pradesh

The Committee obtained views of the Home Secretary on September 21, 1996 on the problems faced by Chakma Tribal Population in Arunachal Pradesh.[16] The Home Secretary informed the Committee briefly as follows:

1. In Arunachal Pradesh, there were only 14,888 Chakmas who had migrated to India in 1964 after their homes were uprooted.
2. The Committee on Petitions of the Tenth Lok Sabha desired that the Government of Arunachal Pradesh may be persuaded not to deny basic facilities like education, trade, ration cards and so on to the migrants for their sustenance. In view of the long stay over 24 years in India as refugees, the Government should explore the possibility of granting Indian Citizenship to these refugees as far as possible.
3. Between 1964 and 1969, 140,000 Chakmas came into Assam. Out of 140,000, about 15,000 refugees were sent to NEFA now Arunachal Pradesh. Loans and land have been given by the Government to the Chakmas of Arunachal Pradesh and State Government at one point itself recommended that these people should be given citizenship.

---

15 *Ibid.*

16 Rajya Sabha Committee on Petitions, no. 9, pp. 6-8.

4. The Government of India took the stand that the Chakmas and Hajongs had been there for so many years from 1964. Now it is 1996 and they should be granted citizenship. The State Government is not cooperating.

5. In October, 1994 complaint regarding stoppage of ration card, ban on employment and economic blockade to the Chakma settlements was made to the National Human Rights Commission.

6. The National Human Rights Commission had asked the State Government to submit the Report but no report has been submitted till date.

7. The Supreme Court heard the case of complaint and passed an interim order on November 2, 1995 that they were not citizens because no citizenship had been granted but they were entitled to citizenship under a particular section of the Citizenship Act.

8. The Supreme Court directed in the interim order that even if they were not citizens, their lives and limbs must be protected and they are entitled to their lives and limbs and that they cannot be evicted from their own places.

9. On January 9, 1996, a final order was passed directing the State Government (i) not to take any action to evict them except under due process of law (ii) application for citizenship should be looked into and sent to the Central Government (iii) to give police force, Central Police for the protection of those people on the demand of State Government.

10. A High Level Group was constituted on December 29, 1995 under the control of the Home Minister

of India in which the Chief Minister was also a member to decide and adopt appropriate measures on this particular issue.

11. The Committee could not go to the State because there was no cooperation from the State Government till this review petition has been disposed of by the Supreme Court.

12. The contention of the State Government was that they had not been consulted when these people were settled.

13. The Chief Minister of Arunachal Pradesh agreed that Chakmas could be given citizenship since they had been living in India for the last 30 years but he said that Chakmas should be settled outside his State.

14. In Arunachal Pradesh, their trade licenses have been stopped and their ration cards have been cancelled. Delegations of India and Bangladesh went to a particular area and convinced the tribal people of Arunachal Pradesh to cooperate with the Chakmas.

15. The Bengal Eastern Frontier Regulation, 1873 governed the Inner Line permit in Arunachal Pradesh. According the Regulation, nobody was allowed to enter Arunachal Pradesh without the permission of the State Government.

16. On October 7, 1995, the then Home Minister, S.B. Chavan, made a statement about relaxation of the Inner Line Permit in Arunachal Pradesh.

17. Restricted Area Permit (RAP) from Assam, Meghalaya and Tripura had been removed with effect from May 19, 1995.

Views of the Government of Arunachal Pradesh on the Chakma issue

The Committee undertook a study visit to Itanagar between November 1 and 5, 1996, and heard the views of the State Government of Arunachal Pradesh and Representatives of Chakmas and indigenous people during the course of the study visit. The Committee heard the views of the representatives of State Government of Arunachal Pradesh at Naharlagun on November 2, 1996.[17] The views of the Government of Arunachal Pradesh included:

1. The Chakmas in Arunachal Pradesh may be shifted to places other than the State of Arunachal Pradesh.
2. The Gauhati High Court had declared Chakmas as foreigners, since they had no right to vote.
3. The number of Chakmas in Arunachal Pradesh is about 60,000 as per refugee calculation.
4. For acquiring land in Arunachal Pradesh, one has to be an indigenous person.
5. Land cannot be given to Chakmas under Legislation passed in 1873 and under the existing laws.
6. About 10 schools for Chakma and non-Chakma children are functioning in Miao Sub-division (Diyun Circle) of the Changlang District, in Chowkham Circle of the Lohit District and in Kokila Circle of the Papumpare District. There is no difficulty in running those schools.
7. The people of Arunachal Pradesh have been tolerating the Chakmas for the past 30 years.

17 *Ibid.*, pp. 13-4.

8. There is no political problem in the State.
9. The problem of settlement of Chakma and Hajong Refugees in Arunachal Pradesh arose during the period of 1964-69. During that time, there was no popular Government in Arunachal Pradesh. In 1964, North-East Frontier Agency (NEFA) was administered by the Central Government, through the Governor of Assam. The Indian People have not been consulted on the settlement of Chakmas in Arunachal Pradesh.
10. The customary laws of the indigenous tribal people have been violated and their traditional rights have been encroached upon by allowing settlement of Chakma and Hajong refugees by the Central Government much against their wishes.
11. The indigenous tribal people of Arunachal Pradesh are of the view that the presence of Chakma and Hajong refugees on their soil is a serious threat to their own survival, their age-old customs and traditions and also the peace.
12. There is nothing common between the tribal people of Arunachal Pradesh and the Chakma refugees.
13. Under the Constitution of India, Arunachal Pradesh has been given special status.
14. The Chakma and Hajong refugees hail from Chittagong Hill Tracts and Maimen Singh District respectively of erstwhile East Pakistan (now Bangladesh).
15. Arunachal Pradesh, the youngest State of the Union of India, has been the most peaceful State in the North-Eastern Region of the country. There

is Chakma lobby in Delhi. They go to Minister for assistance and they have association in Delhi. They also go to the Human Rights Commission.

16. A day will come when Chakmas will be in majority, and indigenous tribal people of Arunachal Pradesh will be in minority.

National Human Right Commission vs. State of Arunachal Pradesh and Union of India

The stand of the Centre to give citizenship rights to the Chakmas of Arunachal Pradesh is also related to the Supreme Court's judgement on the case of National Human Right Commission vs. State of Arunachal Pradesh and Union of India. The judgement was delivered on January 9, 1996 in following words:

> "There is no doubt that Chakmas who migrated from East Pakistan (now Bangladesh) in 1964 first settled down in the State of Assam and shifted to areas which now fall within the State of Arunachal Pradesh. They have settled there since the last about two and a half decades and raised their families in the said State. Their children have married and they too have had children. Thus, a large number of them were born in the State itself. If a person satisfies the requirements of Section 5 of the Citizenship Act, he/she can be registered as a citizen of India. The procedure to be followed in processing such requests has been outlined in part II of the Rules. According to these Rules, application for registration has to be made in the prescribed form, duly affirmed, to the Collector within whose jurisdiction he resides. Under Rule 9, the Collector is expected to transmit every application under Section 5 (1) (a) of the Act to the Central Government. The Collector has merely to receive the application and forward it to the Central

Government. The DC or Collector, who receives the application should be directed to forward the same to the Central Government to enable it to decide the request on merit. The Supreme Court has further added that no person can be deprived of his life or personal liberty except according to procedure established by law. Thus, the State is bound to protect the life and liberty of every human being, be he a citizen or otherwise. The State is duty bound to protect the threatened group and if it fails to do so, it will fail to perform its Constitutional as well as statutory obligations. The State Government must act impartially and carry out its legal obligations to safeguard the life, health and well-being of Chakmas residing in the State without being inhibited by local politics."

The Supreme Court, accordingly, directed that:

1. The State of Arunachal Pradesh shall ensure that the life and personal liberty of each and every Chakma residing within the State shall be protected and any attempt to forcibly evict or drive them out of the State by organized groups shall be repelled.

2. The Chakmas shall not be evicted from their homes and shall not be denied domestic life and comfort therein except in accordance with law.

3. The quit notices and ultimatums issued by the AAPSU and any other group which tantamount to threats to the life and liberty of each and every Chakma should be dealt with by the State of Arunachal Pradesh in accordance with law.

4. The application made for registration as citizen of India by the Chakma shall be forwarded by the Collector or the DC who receives then under

the relevant Rules with or without enquiry, as the case may be to the Central Government for its consideration in accordance with law.

Rajya Sabha Committee on Petitions

The recommendations of the Rajya Sabha Committee on Petitions also played an important role in Centre's taking decision to grant citizenship to the Chakmas. The main recommendations of the Committee in brief are:

1. The Committee have noted that the Chakmas have demanded citizenship, stoppage of their harassment, lifting of ban on their employment, allowing admission to schools, providing medical facilities, trade and business facilities, restoration of ration cards and compensation to the victims of atrocities.
2. The Committee have also noted the contention of the representatives of non-Chakmas and the State Government of Arunachal Pradesh that the presence of Chakmas in Arunachal Pradesh is a threat to their survival, their culture, tradition and peace and that the Chakmas should be evicted from Arunachal Pradesh.
3. The Committee after carefully considering the all facts and the whole issue, has come to the conclusion that Arunachal Pradesh is the only State in the North East which has three International boundaries (with Bhutan, China and Myanmar), which is strategically very important and which has also been relatively calm and insurgency free. It is the sincere desire of the Committee that a reasonable solution is found out to the problems and Justice is done to all.

4. The Committee feels that the spirit of the Indira-Mujib Accord as well as the Judgement of the Supreme Court in the matter may be made applicable to all the affected States for the solution of the problem. As per the Accord, all those Chakmas who came to India prior to March 25, 1971 are to be granted Indian citizenship.

5. The Committee, therefore, recommends that the Chakmas of Arunachal Pradesh who came there prior to March 25, 1971 be granted Indian citizenship. The Committee also recommends that those Chakmas who have been born in India should also be considered for Indian citizenship. The Committee further recommends that the fate of those Chakmas who came to the State after March 25, 1971 be discussed and decided by the Central Government and State Government jointly. The Committees also recommends that all the old applications of Chakmas for citizenship which have either been rejected or withheld by Deputy Commissioners or the State Deputy Commissioner or the State Government continue to block the forwarding of such applications to Central Government, the Central Government may consider to incorporate necessary provision in the Rules (or the Act if so required) whereby it could directly receive, consider and decide the application for citizenship in the case of Chakmas of Arunachal Pradesh. The Committee also recommends that Chakmas be also considered for granting them the status of Scheduled Tribes at the time of granting the citizenship. The Committee would like to earnestly urge upon the Central Government and State Government to ensure that until amicable solution is arrived at, the Chakmas are allowed to stay in Arunachal

Pradesh with full protection and safety, honour and dignity.

Role of Election Commission of India on the inclusion of Chakmas in the Electorate of Arunachal Pradesh

On the basis of a petition filed by the Committee for Citizenship Rights of the Chakmas of Arunachal Pradesh and the Peoples' Union for Civil Liberties before the Delhi High Court in 2000 seeking for directions to the Election Commission of India to enrol all the eligible Chakma voters, the Delhi High Court in a judgement on September 8, 2000, directed the Election Commission of India to enrol the eligible Chakmas and Hajongs into the electoral rolls. On March 29, 2003, the Election Commission of India ordered Special Revision to enrol the Chakma voters pursuant to which more than 11,360 eligible voters have claimed for inclusion of their names. Out of these eligible voters, only 1,497 claimants were accepted and the rest rejected. The State Government of Arunachal Pradesh vide a Cabinet decision on June 14, 2003, deleted the names of these 1,497 Chakma voters from the electoral rolls. The Election Commission of India directed the State government to respect the rule of the law and ensure that the Chakma voters who have been included should not be deleted but the State Government failed to comply with the directions of the Election Commission after which the Commission vide its order dated January 2, 2004, suspended all electoral activities in four Chakma inhabited Assembly constituencies of 14 Doimukh in Papum Pare district, 46 in Chowkham in Lohit district, 49 Bordumsa-Diyun and 50 Miao in Changlang district until the Chakma voters were included in the electoral rolls.[18]

---

18 Committee for Citizenship Rights of the Chakmas of Arunachal Pradesh (CCRCAP), *An Appeal,* New Delhi, August 20, 2004.

On February 24, 2004, the former Chief Minister Mukut Mithi approached the Gauhati High Court against the Election Commission of India by a petition seeking quashing of the Election Commission's order of January 2, 2004. On March 3, 2004, the Election Commission of India by another order asked the State Election Commission of Arunachal Pradesh to include all those 1,497 Chakma voters and publish the electoral roll forthwith.[19]

On March 23, 2005, the Election Commission of India issued additional guidelines for Enumeration to be followed by the electoral authorities in areas having substantial presence of Chakmas.[20] It has ordered that special care has to be taken at the time enumeration in areas having substantial presence of Chakmas namely 14-Doimukh (ST), 46-Chowkham (ST), 49-Bordumsa-Diyun and 50-Miao (ST) assembly constituencies and the following procedures shall be adhered to:

(a) The assembly constituencies where there is a large scale presence of Chakmas should be identified first by the State Government authorities concerned and within such assembly constituencies, the polling areas having a substantial presence of Chakmas should also be likewise identified by those authorities.[21]

(b) At the time of house to house enumeration in these areas, the enumerators shall include in the 'Electoral Card' the names of all the persons as are declared to be adult Indian citizens by the

---

19 Ibid.

20 For details see, The Election Commission of India, *Guidelines No.7.14 (a) to (F) (Additional guidelines for Enumeration in areas having substantial presence of Chakmas,* No.23/ARUN/2004-PLN-II, March 23, 2005.

21 *Ibid.*

head/senior adult member of the household furnishing the information to the Enumerator. He shall also record the date of birth of persons below the Age in the Electoral Card.[22]

(c) The Supervisor concerned on receipt of the enumeration pad and manuscript from the enumerators shall prepare a list of Chakmas separately and submit the same to the ERO.[23]

(d) The ERO concerned, on receipt of the enumeration pad and manuscript from the supervisors shall segregate the names of the Chakmas into two sections, as per the date of birth mentioned in the enumeration pad;

(i) Containing the name of persons who were born in India between January 26, 1950 and July 1, 1987; and in whose case linkage could be established that their parents had migrated to Arunachal Pradesh in 1964, as per the refugee registration records or any other relevant records.

(ii) Containing the names of persons who were born in India between January 26, 1950 and July 1, 1987; and in whose case linkage could not be established that their parents had migrated to Arunachal Pradesh in 1964, as per the refugee registration records or any other relevant records.

e) In respect of those persons whose names have been included in category (d) (i), above, their names shall be straight away included in the draft electoral roll.

22 *Ibid.*

23 *Ibid.*

f) In respect of persons whose linkage could not be established, category (d) (ii), the ERO immediately on receipt of the said list shall cause conduct of local verification to establish the eligibility for enrolment of name in the electoral rolls. The local verification officer shall, among other documentary evidence, rely on the following documents to establish the eligibility of a person of Chakma origin to enrol his or her name in the electoral roll:[24]

(i) Birth certificate showing date of birth and place of birth in India issued by the competent authority;

(ii) School certificate indicating therein date of birth and place of birth in India, and any other certificate which is relevant in the State of Arunachal Pradesh in this regard.

(iii) Only names of those persons whose identities have been established and who were born in India between January 26, 1950 and July 1, 1987 shall be included in the draft electoral rolls.

The disposal of claims and objections received after publication of the draft rolls in the areas as identified above shall be done by following the procedure stated above.[25]

On August 12, 2010, the Government of Arunachal Pradesh wrote to the Election Commission of India requesting it to reinvestigate the inclusion of Chakmas and Hajongs in the electoral rolls. The State Government constituted a nine-member high level committee under

---

24 *Ibid.*

25 *Ibid.*

the Chairmanship of a representative of the Union Home Ministry in June 2010 to examine the Chakma and Hajong settlement report.[26]

Given the above views of the Centre, the Government of Arunachal Pradesh, the Supreme Court, the Rajya Sabha Committee on Petition, and the Election Commission of India in relation to the Chakma issue, it appears that the Centre's approach to resolve the Chakma issue by giving citizenship rights and Scheduled Tribe status to the Chakmas of Arunachal Pradesh has been influenced by various factors such as the permission of the NEFA Administration to settle the Chakma refugees in 1964, the Parliamentary Team's recommendation of 1982, the Assam Accord of 1985, the Indira-Mujib Pact of 1972, the Supreme Court judgement of 1996, the recommendations of the Rajya Sabha Committee on Petitions of 1997, and the role of the Election Commission of India.

On the other hand, the State Government of Arunachal Pradesh rejected the Centre's grant-citizenship approach to resolve the Chakma issue. The State Government opposed the Centre by adopting counter-resolutions demanding the removal of the Chakmas from Arunachal Pradesh on the grounds that indigenous people of Arunachal Pradesh were not consulted about their settlement in 1964, customary laws of the indigenous tribal people have been violated and their traditional rights have been encroached upon by allowing settlement of Chakma and Hajong refugees by the Central Government much against their wishes, land cannot be given to Chakmas under Legislation passed in 1873 and under the existing laws, Chakmas are foreigners so they are not entitled to vote, the indigenous

---

26 For details see, "Khandu moves poll panel after violence," *The Telegraph,* August 12, 2010. p. 17.

tribal people of Arunachal Pradesh are of the view that the presence of Chakma and Hajong refugees on their soil is a serious threat to their own survival, their age-old customs and traditions and also the peace, and under the Constitution of India, Arunachal Pradesh has been given special status. It is also to be noted that the Government of Arunachal Pradesh waged a propaganda war against the Centre as has been evident when the Chief Minister said that if the Centre fails to deport the Chakmas by the year end of 1995, the people of Arunachal will launch agitation for the 'right to self-determination' and the State Government should not be put to blame if the youth of the State went violent against the Chakma settlers.[27] It is also evident from the fact that the Government of Arunachal Pradesh provoked the AAPSU to stage an angry protest against the Rajya Sabha Committee on Petitions when they landed in the helipad of Naharlagun on November 1, 1996.[28]

Table 4.1 Responses of the Union Government over the Chakmas issue

Sl. No.	Responses of the Centre	Percentage of Respondents
1.	To grant citizenship to the Chakmas	39
2.	Expel the Chakmas from India	Nil
3.	To grant citizenship only to those Chakmas born in India	11
4.	Facing opposition from the State Government to grant citizenship to the Chakmas	35
5.	All of the above	Nil
6.	Any other: both the Centre as well as the State Government wanted to keep the issue of granting citizenship to all the Chakmas in Arunachal Pradesh alive for political interests.	15

27 Ashis Chakrabarty, n. 6.

28 Rajya Sabha Committee on Petitions, no. 9, p. 32.

As shown in Table 4.1, 39 percent of the respondents expressed that the Central Government has been affirmative to grant citizenship to the Chakmas of Arunachal Pradesh. No respondents said that the Central Government ever wanted to expel the Chakmas from India. 11 percent of the respondents expressed the view that the Centre had given citizenship only to those Chakmas who were born in India. Another 35 percent said that the Centre has been facing opposition from the State Government of Arunachal Pradesh to grant citizenship to the Chakmas. However, 15 percent of the respondents expressed that both the Centre as well as the State Government wanted to keep the issue of granting citizenship to all the Chakmas in Arunachal Pradesh alive for political interests.

In view of the discussion, it has been seen that the citizenship issue of the Chakmas in Arunachal Pradesh has had serious ramifications on Centre-State relations resulting in a continuous arguments and conflict between the Union Government and the State Government of Arunachal Pradesh. It is also important to note that the conflict between the Union Government of India and the Government of Arunachal Pradesh prompted the rise of ethno-centric politics and ethnic polarization in Arunachal Pradesh which has been examined in the next chapter.

CHAPTER - V

Chakma Issue and Ethno-Politics in Arunachal Pradesh

In the foregoing chapter the conflicting views of the Centre and the Government of Arunachal Pradesh on the Chakma citizenship issue resulting in Centre-State conflict have been examined and it has been seen that the Centre-State conflict provoked the process of ethnic polarization in Arunachal Pradesh. In this chapter, the nature of ethno-politics in Arunachal Pradesh developed in relation to the perceived threats posed by the Chakmas has been examined. The role of the All Arunachal Pradesh Students' Union (AAPSU), the Peoples' Referendum Rally and the various political parties in ethnic mobilization programmes with the Chakma issue has also been examined. However, before discussing the rise of ethno-politics in Arunachal Pradesh in relation to the Chakmas, it is pertinent to have a brief discussion on the meaning and definition of ethnic.

As discussed in the first chapter that ethnic politics is an art of ethnic mobilization often in a relational framework between the native ethnic groups and the outsiders such as refugees. Ethnic politics has been shaped by constraints imposed by outsiders. Thus, the internal 'we' (*ethnos* in Greek) has been distinguished from the external 'aliens' (*ethnikos* in Greek). Where no relevant outsiders existed, the necessity for ethnic politics disappeared. The need of ethnic politics arose only when the strange, threatening, competitive outsiders had been confronted.[1] Ethnicity as politics has been meaningful only in such a relational framework. Further, in ethnic politics, outsiders have been viewed negatively as threats to generate political interests and internal coherence. In that sense, ethnic politics meant cultural mobilization of the *ethnos* or 'we' in relation to *ethnikos* or 'others.'[2] On the other hand, ethnic politics also referred to politics of assertion on the part of 'others' protesting the domination of the native elites.

Ethnicity has been referred to a state of common consciousness of shared origins and traditions.[3] it is a sense of ethnic identity, which has been defined by George de Vos as consisting of the 'subjective, symbolic or emblematic use' by a group of people of any aspect of culture in order to differentiate themselves from other groups.'[4] An ethnic group that used cultural symbols is a subjectively self-conscious community that establishes criteria for inclusion into and exclusion from the group.

1 Milton Jecob Esman, *Ethnic Politics*, (New York: Cornell University Press, 1994), p. 1.

2 For details see, Iris Marion Young, *Justice and Politics of Difference*, (Princeton NJ: Princeton University Press, 1990), pp. 2-10.

3 Iain McLean and Alistair McMillan (eds.), *Oxford Concise Dictionary of Politics,* (New York: Oxford University Press, 2009), p. 177.

4 For details see, George de Vos, "Ethnic Pluralism," in George de Vos and Lola Romanucci-Ross (eds.), *Ethnic Identity: Cultural Continuities and Change,* (California: Mayfield Publishing Co., 1975), p. 16.

The movement from ethnic category to community is a process that may involve such changes as the creation of a self-conscious language community out of a group of related speakers, the formation of a caste association from a caste category or a community of believers from the followers of a particular religious leader. The final stage in the transformation of ethnic groups involves the articulation and acquisition of social, economic and political rights for the members of the group or for the group as a whole. In so far as an ethnic community succeeds by its own efforts in achieving and maintaining group rights through political action and political mobilization, it goes beyond ethnicity and community to establish itself as a nationality.[5]

Ethnicity can incorporate several forms of collective identity, including cultural, religious, national and sub-cultural forms. A distinction may be drawn between cultural ethnicity and political ethnicity. The former refers to a belief in a shared language, religion or other such cultural values and practices. The latter refers to the political awareness or mobilization of a group on a real or assumed ethnic basis.[6]

Ethno-Demographic History of Arunachal Pradesh

Arunachal Pradesh is presently inhabited by about twenty two major tribes and numerous sub-tribes who are said to be Sino-Tibetan by origin.[7] All of these tribes are Scheduled Tribes.[8] But they are distinct from each

5 Paul R Brass, *Ethnicity and Nationalism – Theory and Comparison,* (New Delhi: Sage Publications, 1991), pp. 22-24.

6 For details see, Werner Sollars (ed.), *The Invention of Ethnicity,* (New York: Oxford University Press, 1989), pp. 1-10.

7 N. N. Osik, *A Brief History of Arunachal Pradesh,* (New Delhi: Omsons Publications, 1986), p. 4.

8 S. D. Jha, *The Wealth of Arunachal Pradesh,* (Delhi: Mittal Publications, 1985), p. 68.

other due to their separate geographical, social and religious boundaries. Each of them evolved certain distinctive characteristics in language, dress and customs.[9] As far as language is concerned, there are as many as fifty distinct languages in addition to innumerable dialects and sub-dialects. Although boundaries between their languages often correlated with their divisions, for example, the Apatani and the Nishi are both socially and linguistically distinct, but alterations in their identity and grouping over time have now led to some complications, for example, the Galo is and has seemingly always been linguistically distinct from the Adi, their earlier grouping and alignment made them emerge as the Adi Gallong tribe, the problem of which has only recently been dissolved.[10] The majority of languages spoken in Arunachal Pradesh today belong to a single branch of Tibeto-Burman language family called Tani. The Tani languages are not only spoken in Arunachal Pradesh but also in modern-day Assam and Tibet.

As shown in Table 5.1, Arunachal Pradesh is predominantly inhibited by the Scheduled Tribe population. During 1981 Census, the proportion of Scheduled Tribe population may be accounted for in relation to final total population in Arunachal Pradesh. Table 5.1 transpires that the proportion of Scheduled Tribe population to total population is 91.68 percent in Upper Subansiri which is the highest amongst all the nine districts.

---

9 For details see, Government of Arunachal Pradesh, *http:arunachal pradesh.nic.in/peole.htm.*

10 J. N. Chowdhury, *Indian Historical Researches, Arunachal Pradesh: From Frontier Tracts to Union Territory,* Vol. 39, (New Delhi: Cosmo Publications, 1987), pp. 30-31.

Table 5.1 District-wise Total Population and Scheduled Tribe (ST) Population, 1981

Sl. No.	Districts	Total Population	Total (St) Population	Percentage
1	West Kameng	63,302	41,963	66.9
2	East Kameng	42,736	37,286	87.25
3	Lower Subansiri	112,650	87,605	77.77
4	Upper Subansiri	39,410	36,131	91.68
5	West Siang	74,164	62,323	84.03
6	East Siang	70,451	50,720	71.99
7	Dibang Velley	30,978	15,044	48.56
8	Lohit	69,498	30,130	43.35
9	Tirap	128,650	79,957	62.15
	Total	**631,839**	**441,167**	**69.82**

Source: Census of India, 1981, Series 25, Arunachal Pradesh (New Delhi: Government of India Press, n. d.). Also S. D. Jha, *The Wealth of Arunachal Pradesh,* (Delhi: Mittal Publications, 1985), p. 72.

The lowest percentage proportion of Scheduled Tribe population to total population is noted in the district of Lohit. In Dibang Valley also the Scheduled Tribe population is noted to be 48.56 percent only. In two districts of East Kameng and West Siang, the scheduled tribe population is noted 87.25 percent and 84.03 percent respectively during 1981 head counting. Keeping the above point in view, the districts of West Kameng and Tirap may be bracketed together with 66.29 per cent and 62.15 per cent Scheduled Tribe population to total respective populations. Similarly, the scheduled tribe population enumerates 77.77 per cent in Lower Subansiri and 71.99 per cent in East Siang to respective total population. In view of the above, the percentage of scheduled tribe population in relation to total population works out to 69.82 in Arunachal Pradesh during 1981 census.

Arunachal Pradesh can be roughly divided into a set of semi-distinct cultural spheres on the basis of tribal identity, language and religion: the Tibetic area bordering Bhutan in the west, the Tani area in the centre of the State, the Mishmi area to the east of the Tani area, the Singpho and the Tangsa area bordering Burma, and the "Naga" area to the south, which also borders Burma. In between there are transition zones, such as the area of the Aka, the Miji and the Sherdukpen, which provided sort of a "buffer" between the Tibetan Buddhist tribes and the animist Tani hill tribes. In addition, there are isolated peoples scattered throughout the state, such as the Sulung.[11]

Within each of these cultural spheres, there are populations of related tribes speaking related languages and sharing similar traditions. In the Tibetan origin area, one finds large numbers of the Monpa tribes, with several sub-tribes speaking closely related but mutually incomprehensible languages. Within the Tani area, major tribes include the Nishi, the Bangni, the Tagin and even the Hill Miri. The Apatani also live among the Nishi, but are distinct. In the centre, one finds predominantly Galo people, with the major sub-groups of Lare and Pugo. In the east, one finds the Adi, with many sub-tribes including Padam, Pasi, Minyong, and Bokar, among others. Milang, while also falling within the general "Adi" sphere, are in many ways quite distinct. Moving east, the Idu, Miju and Digaru make up the "Mishmi" cultural-linguistic area, which may or may not form a coherent historical grouping.[12]

Moving on to the southeast of Arunachal Pradesh, the Tai Khamti are linguistically distinct from their

11 *Ibid.,* pp. 23-35.

12 *Ibid.,* pp. 25-34.

neighbours and culturally distinct from the majority of other Arunachalee tribes; they are religiously similar to the Chakma refugees in the districts of Lohit, Changlang, Dibang and Papump are. They also exhibit considerable convergence with the Singpho and the Tangsa tribes of the same area, all of which are also found in Burma. Finally, the Nocte and the Wancho exhibit cultural and possibly also linguistic affinities to the tribes of Nagaland, which they border.[13]

In Table 5.2, the names and population of the major ethnic groups of Arunachal Pradesh have been figured out. It is to be noted here that the identification of tribes in Arunachal Pradesh varied from time to time. The 1961 report of the Commission for Scheduled Areas and Scheduled Tribes mentions of about 29 main and 41 sub-tribes in Arunachal Pradesh.[14] The Census report of India, 1961, put the figure at 22 major and over 60 sub-tribes, whereas the Census of 1971 recorded a collective of 110 tribes in total existed in the State, while again the Census of 1981 put the figure at 106 in total.[15] The Government of Arunachal Pradesh maintains that there are only 20 major tribal groups in the State. However, the number of tribes produced in Table 5.2 is on the basis of the Census report of India, 1961.

According to the provisional Census report of India, 2011, the total population of Arunachal Pradesh is 1,382,611 of which male and female are 720,232 and 662,379 respectively and are scattered over 12 towns and 3649 villages.

13 For details see, Usha Sharma, *Discovery of North-East India*, (Delhi: Mittal Publications, 2005), pp. 55-65.

14 For details see, *Report of the Scheduled Areas and Scheduled Tribes Commission*, Vol. 1, 1960-61, p. 476.

15 For details see, Census of India, 1961, 1971, 1981.

Table 5.2 Major Ethnic Groups of Arunachal Pradesh and their Population

Ethnic Groups	Population	Percentage
Adi	82, 357	24.47
Aka or Hrusso	2,257	0.67
Apatani	10,949	3.25
Bangni	26,436	7.86
Bokar	2,472	0.74
Digaru	5,149	1.53
Hill Miri	2,533	0.75
Idu	2,207	0.66
Khamti	2,556	0.76
Khamba	1,133	0.37
Memba	2,497	0.74
Miji	2,079	0.62
Miju	7,719	2.29
Monpa	21,982	6.53
Nishi	35,089	10.43
Nocte	19,353	5.75
Sherdukpen	1,154	0.34
Singpho	983	0.29
Sulung	1,519	0.45
Tagin	24,283	7.21
Tangsa	10,396	3.08
Wancho	23,393	6.95

Source: Census of India, 1961; *Arunachal: 1947-72*, published from the office of the Director of Information and Public Relations, Shillong, n. d., p. 54.

In 2001, the total population of the State was 1,097,968 in which males were 579,941 while females were 518,027. The State has the lowest density of 17 persons per square kilometre which was 13 persons per square kilometre in 2001. The total population growth during this decade is 25.92 percent while in the previous decade it was 26.21 percent. The population of Arunachal Pradesh forms 0.11 percent of India in 2011 almost equal to the figure what was in 2001.[16]

Thus, it may be noted that the tribes of Arunachal are so numerous and are culturally so distinct from one another that each of them can at best be termed as a distinct ethnic group. These tribes are yet to develop a common consciousness of shared origins and traditions, self-conscious and cohesive entities like communities as defined. Nor can they claim to have established themselves as a nationality since a distinct Arunachali identity has not emerged because of the cultural diversities within the State. The absence of complex networks of kinship and marital alliances at wider territorial level of Arunachal Pradesh are also typical features of caste societies deterred ethnic nationality formation in Arunachal Pradesh.[17]

Keeping ethno-historical and demographic background of the Arunachali society in view, now the role of the AAPSU, the Peoples' Referendum Rally and the various political parties in ethnic mobilization and politicization vis-à-vis the perceived threats of the Chakmas has been examined hereunder.

AAPSU Movement and Ethnic Politics

Politics of student movement in Arunachal Pradesh often followed an ethnic path, particularly in relation to the Chakma issue. The ethnic role of the AAPSU is rooted in its history itself. In fact, the very reason behind the emergence of the AAPSU is to raise the grievances

---

16 For details see, "Census of India: Provisional Population Tables - Census 2011," *censusindia.gov.in.*

17 N. K. Das, *Ethnic Identity, Ethnicity and Social Stratification in North-East India,* (New Delhi: Inter-India Publications, 1989), p. 245.

and aspirations of the indigenous people of Arunachal Pradesh. Scholars have observed that the role played by the AAPSU is distinct in many aspects. One aspect is that it has not been stereotypical to students' interests within the college campus only. It has engaged itself in social cause and politics to bring transformation.[18] One of the fundamental premises to be considered is that although the AAPSU is an organization of students, it is at the same time exposed to the dominant tribal intelligentsia of the State. In most cases, the dominant class of Arunachal Pradesh employ their hegemony to motivate students under the banner of the AAPSU to act in a particular manner for ethnic mobilization, as in the case of outsider Chakmas.[19]

To begin with, the Preamble of the AAPSU Constitution declares that the objective of the AAPSU is to promote unity and fraternity among the students in particular and the people of the State in general, to explore and exploit the energy of the student community of the State in the greater interest of the society and to preserve and promote the tradition and culture of the people of Arunachal Pradesh. It appears that the phrase 'people of Arunachal Pradesh' has been used in a loose manner because the state is inhabited by 26 major tribal communities, each with a distinct tradition and culture as well as non-tribals from various parts of India. The

---

18 For details see, S. Dutta, 'Student Movement in Arunachal Pradesh,' in A. K. Baruah (ed.), *Student Power in North-East India Understanding Student Movements,* (New Delhi: Regency Publications, 2002), p. 205.

19 Susmita Sen Gupta, "Ethnic Issues and All Arunachal Students' Union", *Proceedings of the North East India Political Science Association,* Seventh Annual Conference, (North-Eastern Hill University, Tura Campus, December, 1997), p. 45.

AAPSU cannot claim to be a champion of the interests of all these communities. Rather, it seems to represent the interests of the dominant ethnic groups in the state. It may be argued, therefore, that an element of ethnicity is implicit in the Preamble to the AAPSU Constitution, even though it does not spell out explicitly.[20]

The factor of perceived demographic threat of the Chakmas brought a drastic change in the nature of the AAPSU movement and politics. Initially, the AAPSU movement was development oriented and its demands were centred onproblems like establishment of higher educational institutions, change of the medium of instruction from Assamese to English, to upgrade the NEFA administration to Union Territory, and reservation of seats in various Science and Technical Institutions.[21] As Talom Rukbo, one of the founder members of the AAPSU, remarked, "it must be remembered that the students union of the early days never launched strikes in the present manner . . . they used to give thumping pressure to the Government on any demand if not satisfied, but in a reasonable and peaceful manner."[22] However, in 1979, the AAPSU altered its objectives. Unlike before, it started to draw attention to such problems like the State boundary dispute with Assam, cultural integrity of the tribal people of the State and the presence of non-Arunachalee residents in the State, particularly fear of demographic subjugation by the larger number of Chakma refugees in the State. In April, 1980, a 48-hour *bandh* was called by the AAPSU on the following charter of demands:[23]

---

20 *Ibid.*, p. 40.

21 S. Dutta, n. 18, p. 205.

22 *Ibid.*, p. 206.

23 N. K. Das, n. 17, p. 249.

1. Solution of boundary disputes between Assam and Arunachal Pradesh;
2. Detection and deportation of foreign nationals from Arunachal Pradesh;
3. Withdrawal of land allotment permit and trade licences from the non-Arunachalis; and
4. Effective check against further infiltration of foreign nationals.

Another factor that influenced the AAPSU to launch its movement on ethnic direction over the Chakma issue was the famous Assam movement on the foreign national issue. In the early 1980s, ethnic issues started to dominate the politics of Assam when the All Assam Student's Union (AASU) launched its ethno-cultural movement against the foreign nationals in Assam. Having influenced by the ethnic movement in Assam, the AAPSU too launched it movement on the Chakma issue in 1982 which marked the beginning of ethno-politics of the AAPSU movement in Arunachal Pradesh.[24] On August 26, 1985, the AAPSU adopted a detailed resolution on the demographic threat posed by the Chakmas in Arunachal Pradesh and submitted a memorandum to the Government of Arunachal Pradesh demanding immediate withdrawal of the Chakma refugees stating the reason that the steady growth of the Chakma population has threatened the demographic picture of the area.

Considering the fact that the Chakma migrants formed a sizeable non-local population as compared to the rather small indigenous population of Arunachal Pradesh all of whom are Scheduled Tribes, it seems that migration may have led to certain demographic changes

24 *Ibid.*, pp. 209-10.

in the State. Such changes are both real and perceived. For an understanding of the demographic structure of Arunachal Pradesh, we propose to take a glance at the density of population in North-East India as well as a look at the percentage of Scheduled Tribe population in Arunachal Pradesh. In this context, it is important to note that among all the states in the North-East, Arunachal Pradesh is the largest in terms of area, but the density of population in the State is only 17 persons per square kilometre as per the 2011 Census which not only ranks lowest in the North-East, but also in India. This may be interpreted to mean that the overall impact of Chakma migrants may not be devastating as perceived by the native population in Arunachal. It may also be noted that in 1981, indigenous tribals constituted the majority of the population of Arunachal in all the districts except in Lohit and Dibang Valley. In contrast, in 1991, Scheduled Tribes were not in a majority in Lohit, Dibang Valley and Changlang districts. This indicates some changes in the population structure during 1982-1991. Moreover, there was a slight, but steady decline in the tribal population in all the districts. The most spectacular development, however, was the sharp fall in the percentage of tribal population in Changlang district. It appears, therefore, that the presence of the Chakmas has brought about a significant change in the demographic structure in Changlang district only, not in the State as a whole.[25] While there is some confusion about the exact number of Chakmas and Hajongs settled in Arunachal, it appears that the threat posed by the Chakma refugees on the demographic balance in the State has been exaggerated to a great extent.

---

25 For details see, Statistical Pocket Book Arunachal Pradesh, 1985, Directorate of Economics and Statistics, Government of Arunachal Pradesh, Shillong, 1985.

But the fact remains that the threat, whether imagined or real, on the demographic structure in Arunachal is considered to have consequences for the culture of the indigenous people. This was highlighted by resource persons in a workshop on right of self-determination and self-government of indigenous peoples held in Itanagar on April 1-2, 1995.[26] It was observed that indigenous people who have their own distinctive identity, culture, ethos, own way of life and self-governing system, were suffering from political, economic and social discrimination and were being systematically marginalized and pushed to non-dominant entity in the present political system of India which is alien to them. It was also felt that the unabated influx of foreigners and also internal migration from other parts of the country and settlement of refugees in traditional homelands of indigenous peoples were increasingly threatening to outnumber the indigenous population in their own homelands. The speakers emphasized that the Chakma and Hajong Refugees were diluting the indigenous character of natives to the great danger of extinction. It was therefore recommended that in order to save the natives and their identity, all the migrants must be expelled from Arunachal Pradesh. On the other hand, one cannot dispute the contention that it was the Government of India which settled these refugees in the then NEFA in the mid 1960s. So four decades of continuous stay have led the Chakmas to claim what they call an "occupational right". It appears, therefore that even if the nationality of the Chakma is questioned, but their right to sustain themselves cannot be disputed,

---

26 North East Indigenous Tribal Peoples' Forum (NEITPF), *Summary of Workshop on Indigenous Tribal Peoples' Right of Self-Determination and Self -Government,"* Itanagar, April 1-2, 1995, pp.1-2.

at least on humanitarian ground. But the problem arises when this right comes in conflict with the right of indigenous tribes who have a distinct way of life.[27]

The factor of demographic threat of the Chakmas dominated the grass roots ethno-politics of Arunachal Pradesh again in 1994 when the AAPSU embarked on an agitational programme against Chakmas. Things reached a flash point when on August 1, 1994 the AAPSU issued "Quit Arunachal Notice" to the Chakmas to leave the state peacefully by September 30, 1994. As a follow-up of their notice, the AAPSU organized rallies in different parts of the state including Kokila and Miao, where Chakmas are concentrated.[28] In that connection, the General Secretary of AAPSU, Domin Loya, once pointed out that the Chakma foreign nationals should be made aware that they were given shelter on humanitarian grounds and that they should not take undue advantage of the hospitality shown by the people of this State. It appears that the AAPSU leadership is aware of the compulsions that led the Government of India to accommodate the Chakmas in the then NEFA. At the same time, an intolerant attitude towards the Chakma migrants is clearly perceptible. Such an attitude may perhaps be accounted for by two factors. First, in the perception of AAPSU, the migrants form a sizeable non-local population *vis-à-vis* the small indigenous population and secondly, the AASU seems to have articulated the concern of the indigenous tribal society about protection of its rights to land and resources and its natural aversion to sharing these with non-locals. Viewed in this context, the ethnic issue taken up by the AAPSU acquired the dimension of a nativist movement

---

27 Susmita Sen Gupta, n. 19, p. 44.

28 For details see, "Amnesty urges Rao to protect Chakmas," *The Statesman*, New Delhi, October 10, 1994.

because it highlights the conflicts between the sons of the soil or natives and the Chakma migrants. Expressing disapproval of the manner in which the migrants have been asserting their rights, the AAPSU President, Takam Sanjoy, stated, "When we have fed them, they want to sleep. When we allowed them to sleep, they want to extend their claims." The Student leader was critical of the fact that the Chakmas could dare demand citizenship by approaching the Supreme Court.

Some of the allegations of the AAPSU against the Chakmas are that they are creating serious law and order problems, threatening the demographic balance, peaceful coexistence and the very identity of the indigenous people of the State. Their illegal settlement in the State, demand for permanent citizenship rights and misrepresentation of facts and figures to various forums, the AAPSU alleged, have created fear among the indigenous Arunachali people and tarnished the image of the State. The AAPSU further alleges that the Chakmas have dishonoured the verdict of the Supreme Court which is highly objectionable.

The AAPSU's allegation regarding the illegal settlement of refugees sounds paradoxical because it was the Indian Government which accommodated the Chakmas and Hajongs under a specific scheme in the then NEFA. It is interesting to explore the grounds on which the Chakmas have demanded citizenship rights. It was pointed out by the Chakma leaders that the Assam Accord of 1985 (Section 6-A of the Citizenship Act of 1955) on the foreigners' issue clearly stated that all persons of Indian origin who have settled in Assam on or before January 1, 1966, are deemed to be citizens of India. By pointing out that the Chakmas and Hajongs came to India way back in 1964, they argue that there is no reason as to why the provisions of the Assam Accord should not be made applicable in the State of Arunachal Pradesh also and citizenship conferred to the Chakmas and Hajongs accordingly as Arunachal Pradesh was constitutionally a part of Assam till 1972. The Chakmas, therefore, asserted that they have the legitimate right to Indian citizenship.[29]

On the other side, it may be noted that protests against the granting of citizenship to Chakmas spearheaded by the AAPSU seemed to have been based on the ruling of the Gauhati High Court and the Supreme Court on the Constitutional status of the migrants. Referring to the fundamental rights enjoyed by the foreigners, the Supreme Court held in its judgement in the State of Arunachal Pradesh versus Khudiram Chakma in paragraph-33 that even a foreigner has a fundamental right, but that right is confined only to Article 21 and does not include the right to move freely throughout and to reside and stay in any part of the territory of India as conferred under Article 19 (1)(d) and (c). Such a right, according to the Supreme Court, is available only to citizens. It held that foreigners cannot invoke Art 14 to get the same right denied to them under Article 19 since Article 14 cannot operate in regard to a right specifically withheld from non-citizens.[30]

The difference in the rate of literacy between the Chakmas and natives played a crucial role in the ethno-politics of the AAPSU movement. A look at the literacy rate of the Chakmas *vis-à-vis* the natives will make it clear. According to one estimate, the literacy rate among the Chakmas is 70 to 75 percent as compared to 52 per

---

29 Committee for Citizenship Rights of the Chakmas of Arunachal Pradesh (CCRCAP), *An Appeal,* New Delhi, August 20-22, 1994.

30 For details see, State of Arunachal Pradesh vs. Khudiram Chakma [1993] Rd-SC 236 (27 April 1993).

cent of the natives of Arunachal Pradesh. If this estimate is treated as authoritative, it may be argued that the Chakmas with their high literacy rate are likely to emerge as serious competitors on the employment front.

Economic factors also appeared to be an important determinant of the conflict between the Chakma and the natives. The Chakmas grow rice and wheat in the fertile low-lying areas of Miao Sub-division and maize, vegetables and horticultural products in the uplands. They are also the main suppliers of agricultural produce to Miao and other towns in Changlang district. Thus, the Chakmas appeared to be highly enterprising and are doing reasonably well in the field of agriculture. Resentment of the locals against the prosperous migrants was articulated by the students when the Changlang district unit of AAPSU enforced an "economic blockade" upon the Chakmas calling upon the natives not to buy anything from the refugees. Such a step taken by the AAPSU had a negative fall-out on the economy of the State and the most visible consequence was a shortage of fresh vegetables in market.[31]

As discussed in chapter two, a new phase of the AAPSU movement on the Chakma issue began from 2004 when 1,497 Chakmas have been conferred citizenship rights and were allowed by the Election Commission of India to participate in the Assembly elections held on May 5, 2004, in response to which the AAPSU called for a civil disobedience movement and urged upon the people of Arunachal Pradesh to boycott the elections followed by a 48-hour bandh all over the State.[32] In 2009, the AAPSU has filed a Public Interest Litigation (PIL) in Gauhati

---

31 Susmita Sen Gupta, No. 19, p. 44.

32 For details see, Ripunjoy Das, "Chakmas and Hajongs today scripted a new chapter in the electoral history of Arunachal Pradesh," *The Telegraph,* Calcutta, May 6, 2004.

High Court terming the Election Commission's guidelines to include the names of Chakma refugees in the electoral roll for the Lok Sabha elections as illegal.[33]

It appeared from the discussion that the ethnic issues taken up by the AAPSU at the background of Chakma issue sustained by several factors that vary from an actual threat to indigenous identity to a perception of fear that the AAPSU seems to have injected in the popular psyche. The actual threat comes from the fact that the Chakmas by their higher literacy rate vis-à-vis the indigenous tribals and by their entrepreneurship appeared to have earned a place for them in Arunachal. As things stand at present, the natives are facing a stiff competition from Chakmas in the field of education, employment and productive activities, particularly in agriculture. Viewed in this context, apprehensions expressed by the AAPSU have a genuine ground. But, on the other hand, Census figures about the population structure and the density of population in Arunachal suggest that the demographic balance in the State has not been affected to an alarming extent due to the settlement of Chakmas and other migrants in Arunachal Pradesh. As noted before, the Union Government cited the Indira-Mujib Pact of 1972 as the basis for the proposal of granting citizenship to the Chakmas. On the whole, the Chakma issue has got tangled in too many legal complexities and has been fuelled by allegations and counter allegations from both the Chakmas and the Arunachalis. The humanitarian angle of the Chakma issue has been relegated to the background as a consequence. Under the banner of the AAPSU, the educated elite in Arunachal, seemed to have utilised their hegemony for mass mobilization by not simply

33 For details see, "Students' union files PIL against Chakmas." *The Telegraph, Guwahati,* June 11, 2009.

raising the ethnic issues, but also by arousing popular sentiment against Chakmas who are alleged to have emerged as stiff contenders in the field of education, employment, and other economic pursuits. Such a posture adopted by the AAPSU is also likely to benefit them most in the sense that by projecting the Chakmas as a rival community vis-à-vis indigenous Arunachalis, they may hope to gain considerable political mileage over political parties in Arunachal, particularly the Congress and its subsequent reincarnation, the Arunachal Congress. Ethnic issues have thus become an important component of grass-roots politics in Arunachal Pradesh and the AAPSU has certainly emerged as a major player in this politics in the absence of any significant organization capable of articulating demands of the society on such issues vigorously and effectively.

Peoples' Referendum Rally of Arunachal Pradesh

The demand made in an Appeal by the Peoples' Referendum Rally of Arunachal Pradesh on September 20, 1995, as:

> "The refugee problem is a burning issue in our peaceful State of Arunachal Pradesh. Their demand for permanent citizenship rights is creating panic among the bona fide people. Considering the serious nature of the problem.... We demand Chakma refugees to quit Arunachal Pradesh,"[34]

reflected ethno-politics by the native Arunachalis.

According to Table 5.3, 58 percent of the respondents expressed that the Chakma issue played a positive role in creating a feeling of oneness among the Arunachalis

---

34 Organising Committee Peoples' Referendum Rally, *An Appeal*, Naharlagun, Arunachal Pradesh, September 20, 1995.

to resist the demographic and political threats with the presence of Chakmas.

Table 5.3 Unity among the Native Tribes of Arunachal Pradesh over the Chakma Issue

Sl. No.	Unity of native Arunachalis	Percentage of Respondents
1.	Has Chakma issue brought unity among Arunachalis?	58
2.	Has Chakma issue brought disunity among Arunachalis?	Nil
3.	Both of the above	Nil
4.	Any other: Chakma issue provided opportunity for the tribal elites of Arunachal Pradesh to fulfil their political interests.	42

No respondent expressed that the threat of the Chakmas brought disunity among the native Arunachalis. No respondents expressed that the Chakma issue led to both unity and disunity among the native Arunachalis. However, 42 percent said that the Chakma issue provided opportunity for the tribal elites of Arunachal Pradesh to fulfil their political goals.

Thus, it can said that the perceived threats of the Chakmas have been politicized by the tribal elite of Arunachal Pradesh under the banner of the AAPSU for ethnic mobilization to achieve their interests as the Peoples' Referendum Rally provided the evidence.

CHAPTER - VI

Conclusion

Forced migration and resettlement of people from one country to another is a crude phenomenon of contemporary human history. Much of its causes originate from the post-colonial fallible nation-state system. As the tale of displacement of the Chakmas from the CHT and their post-refugee life in Arunachal Pradesh demonstrate how deeply it lies in the pattern of religious persecution and fitful development project such as massive dam construction at the origin state of Pakistan and soon nowhere people at the receiving state of India. The partition of British India changed the identity, citizenship status, and natural belongingness to earth of many traditional social groups like the Chakmas. They are now stateless without citizenship in Arunachal Pradesh.

This chapter provides the major findings and observations of the study which are as follows:

1. The exodus of the Chakmas was caused by two clandestine government plans: 1) persecution plan of the Pakistan Government, and 2) plan to buildthe killer Kaptai dam. Had the homeland

of the Chakmas, the CHT, been included in India their life would have been better. They demanded to be in India and still fighting to be in India. They hoisted the Indian national flag at Rangamati until the Pakistan Government seized the CHT on August 21, 1947. India did not take any actions despite help sought. In 1964, the government of Pakistan ended the special status of the CHT. Religious persecution on the Chakmas is continued in more sophisticated manner by today's Bangladesh government. As reported, torture, rape, and false charges on the Chakmas by the Bangladesh army is everyday affair. Therefore, further exodus of the Chakmas cannot be brushed aside. The brunt would be on India.

2. The Chakma citizenship issue in Arunachal Pradesh appears to be an open mystery. They were resettled by the Central Government of India in consultation with the then NEFA administration and local leaders in demarcated areas. All post-partition and all pre-Bangladesh refugee issues are permanently solved, so why Chakma refugees of 1964 are still denied citizenship in Arunachal? They live in Tripura and Mizoram as dignified citizens. The economic contribution of the Chakmas in the making of Arunachal Pradesh cannot be denied. They have shown skill in cultural assimilation well. They can speak the languages of their immediate neighbors quite well. They speak fluent Assamese too.

3. The presence of the Chakmas in Arunachal was not an issue for three decades (1964-1994). With New Delhi's announcement to grant them citizenship in 1992, they immediately became a significant matter in the politics of the state. A political capital is born.

4. The Chakma citizenship issue has altered the nature of student activism in Arunachal Pradesh from non-violent nature to violent and agitational mode. The educated elite of Arunachal Pradesh under the banner of the AAPSU often used the Chakma issue for mass mobilization.
5. Chakma issue has had a revolutionary impact on party politics of Arunachal. The Congress Party in Arunachal Pradesh got split due to the issue. The then Congress Chief Minister, Gegong Apang, resigned from the INC along with his Cabinet colleagues and formed a new State political party called the Arunachal Congress in 1996 because his own party holding power in Delhi failed to resolve the Chakma issue.
6. The Chakma issue has also invented ethnic-polarization in Arunachal Pradesh affecting the Centre-State relations. Centre's decision to grant citizenship to the Chakmas and for ignoring the rights of the indigenous Arunachalis has generated local resentment against the Centre.
7. The perceived fear of the Chakmas has produced a stimulus-response among the Arunachal's diverse ethnic groups who never had a sense of oneness and unity as they could not understand each other's languages. As records say, there are 24 major tribes and over 100 sub-tribes in the state. Ethnic balance in the state meant only vis-à-vis the Chakmas.

Observations

The study revealed the background and present status of the Chakma issue in the politics of Arunachal Pradesh. In the light of the above findings, the following observations have been drawn towards a permanent solution of the issue.

- It has been observed that the Chakma issue continues to remain unresolved mainly due to the lack of serious measures and political will both on the part of Central and State Governments. It appears that the High Level Committee constituted by the Centre to work out a solution to the problem has long been inactive. If the issue remains unresolved, it may give rise to violent ethnic conflict between the Chakmas and the Arunachali neighbours since socio-political forces of state such as the AAPSU, the Peoples' Referendum Rally and various political parties of Arunachal Pradesh have already politicized the issue for ethnic mobilization and polarization by projecting the Chakmas as demographic and political threat to the native tribes. No solution will come until the issue is de-politicized and from neutral point of view.
- The Chakmas have been living in Arunachal Pradesh for more than half a century now. Therefore, the demand of the State Government and the AAPSU to remove the Chakmas from Arunachal Pradesh seems to be irrational and illogical. After living more than half a century in a land would give any body a natural right to claim the land occupancy as they tilted and used it for survival. Moreover, the Chakmas came from erstwhile East Pakistan which ceased to exist in 1971 with the creation of Bangladesh. More importantly, 60 percent of the present Chakmas in Arunachal Pradesh were actually born in the soil of Arunachal Pradesh and that itself allows them to be natural citizens of the state. Therefore, such a demand of the State Government to expel the Chakmas looks unrealistic except making the issue more complex.

Instead, the Government of Arunachal Pradesh may adopt the same policy to resolve the issue the way the Tibetan refugee issue in the state was solved by granting citizenship to 90 Tibetan refugee families living in Shyo village of Tawang District in 2002.

- Centre's policy to grant citizenship to the Chakmas has been rather too slow and ambivalent. The applications submitted by Chakmas for citizenship to the concerned District Collector's office are rarely forwarded to the Centre for final approval of citizenship. It is therefore, suggested that the Government of India takes a strong measure by declaring the Chakmas as citizens of Arunachal.
- The intellectual elite of Arunachal Pradesh seemed to have exaggerated the demographic and political threat of the Chakmas for political gains rather than finding an intellectual approach for understanding the issue. The educated elite of Arunachal Pradesh can play a significant role to resolve the issue rather than taking political advantage out of it.
- During the fieldwork it has been observed that Chakmas are deprived of basic facilities of human life such as medical treatment, primary education, and trade permission. So far no Chakma is given a Government job in Arunachal Pradesh. Chakmas showed the author some documents like trade licenses, ration cards etc. issued to them earlier. But they said these facilities are presently withdrawn from them.
- If the citizenship status of the Chakmas in Arunachal Pradesh remains unresolved and if the

Government of Arunachal Pradesh, the people of Arunachal Pradesh do not accept them as fellow citizens of the State, there is every possibility of a resistance movement by the Chakmas for a separate autonomy within Arunachal Pradesh. While the entire Arunachal Pradesh is a State of various assimilated tribes came at different points in history like the Khamtis who came from China barely a century and a half ago, what is the problem with the Chakmas who economically contributed to the State more than any other groups. For example, plough and wet land cultivation introduced by the Chakma refugees not only increased food production but also developed trade and commerce with neighboring Assam.

- The political leaders should refrain from giving false statements to remove the Chakmas from Arunachal. They have been making such statements since the 1980s. People of Arunachal should know that it is no more possible to remove them. That is why it is suggested to de-politicize the issue and accept legal and human rights approaches. The Supreme Court's verdict given twice – first in 1996 and then again in 2015 for granting citizenship to the Chakmas should be honored and obeyed by the State of Arunachal Pradesh. In fact, the problem was solved in 1996 itself given the Supreme Court's verdict. Generosity and compassion solved many refugee issues in the world recognizing refugee assimilation and multiculturalism as the order of human civilizations no matter how ethno-centric and xenophobic we are. Here, one must recall what the French philosopher Pierre Joseph Proudhon said, "This land of earth belongs to nobody except to those who till and use it for livelihood."

Bibliography

Primary Sources

Primary sources included the Proceedings of the Arunachal Pradesh Legislative Assembly, Parliamentary debates, Letters of the Members of Parliament, Government Letters, Government Reports, Nongovernment Reports, and Supreme Court Judgment which are as follows.

Proceedings of the Arunachal Pradesh Legislative Assembly

Proceedings of the Arunachal Pradesh Legislative Assembly, First Session, Assembly Secretariat, Naharlagun, (March 24-28, 1997).

Proceedings of the Arunachal Pradesh Legislative Assembly, Third Session, Assembly Secretariat, Naharlagun, (December 21-22, 1995).

Proceedings of the Arunachal Pradesh Legislative Assembly, Sixth Session, Assembly Secretariat, Naharlagun, (January 21-22, 1997).

Proceedings of the Arunachal Pradesh Legislative Assembly, Eighth Session, Assembly Secretariat, Naharlagun, (August 14-15, 1997).

Proceedings of the Arunachal Pradesh Legislative Assembly, Seventh Session, Assembly Secretariat, Naharlagun, (March 6, 26-27, 29, 31, 1997).

Proceedings of the Arunachal Pradesh Legislative Assembly, Ninth Session, Assembly Secretariat, Naharlagun, (March 23-24, 1998).

Proceedings of the Arunachal Pradesh Legislative Assembly, Second Session, Assembly Secretariat, Naharlagun, (March 24-25, 27-28, 2000).

Parliamentary Debates

Lok Sabha, *Grant of Indian Citizenship to Chakma Refugees in Arunachal Pradesh*, Lok Sabha Secretariat, New Delhi, February 27, 1992.

Letters of the Members of Parliament

Letter of L. K. Advani, Member of Parliament, Leader of Opposition, Lok Sabha, to S. B. Chavan, Minister of Home Affairs, Ministry of Home Affairs, Government of India, New Delhi, March 4, 1992.

Letter of Somnath Chatterjee, Member of Parliament, Leader of CPI (M), Lok Sabha, to P. V. Narasimha Rao, Prime Minister of India, Government of India, New Delhi, March 31, 1992.

Letter of P. V. Narasimha Rao, Prime Minister of India, Government of India, to Somnath Chatterjee, Member of Parliament, Leader of CPI (M), Lok Sabha, New Delhi April 8, 1992.

Letter of Chitta Basu, Member of Parliament, Lok Sabha, to P. V. Narasimha Rao, Prime Minister of India, Government of India, New Delhi, March 14, 1992.

Letter of Indrajit Gupta, Member of Parliament, Lok Sabha, to P. V. Narasimha Rao, Prime Minister of India, Government of India, New Delhi, February 18, 1992.

Letter of Swaraj Kaushal, Member of Parliament, Rajya Sabha, to L. K. Advani, Deputy Prime Minister of India, Government of India, New Delhi, July 15, 2003.

Letter of L. K. Advani, Deputy Prime Minister of India, Government of India, to SwarajKaushal, Member of Parliament, Rajya Sabha, New Delhi, September 1, 2003.

Government Letters

Letter D. O. No. 12/16/92/-MZ, Minister of State for Home and Parliamentary Affairs, India, North Block, New Delhi, September 23, 1992.

Letter D. O. No. 13/12/94/-MZ, Minister of State for Home and Parliamentary Affairs, India, North Block, New Delhi, July 7, 1994.

Ministry of Home Affairs (North East Division) on the petition pertaining to the problems being faced by the Chakma Tribal Population in Mizoram and Arunachal Pradesh vide their Office Memo No. 13/15/95-NE September 18, 1996.

Government Reports

Rajya Sabha Committee on Petitions, *Hundred and Fifth Report,* (New Delhi: Rajya Sabha Secretariat, August 14, 1997).

Publication Division of India, *NEFA,* (Delhi: Government of India, n. d. 1965).

Non-government Reports

All Arunachal Chakma Youths' Federation, *A Universal Appeal on the Plight of the Chakmas of Arunachal Pradesh*, Diyun, Tirap District, Arunachal Pradesh, April 11-12, 1981.

All India Chakma Cultural Conference (AICCC), *The Plight of the Chakma in Arunachal Pradesh*, Machmara, Tripura, November 11-12, 1995.

Committee for Citizenship Rights of the Chakmas of Arunachal Pradesh, *An Appeal*, New Delhi, August 8, 1995.

Committee for Citizenship Rights of the Chakmas of Arunachal Pradesh, *An Appeal*, New Delhi, August 8, 1995.

Organising Committee Peoples' Referendum Rally, *An Appeal*, Naharlagun, Arunachal Pradesh, September 20, 1995.

Peoples' Rights Organization (PRO), *The Question of Indian Citizenship Rights of the Stateless Chakmas and Hajongs of Arunachal Pradesh*, (New Delhi, September, 1992).

Supreme Court Judgment

Supreme Court of India, National Human Rights Commission Versus State of Arunachal Pradesh, Original Civil Jurisdiction, Writ Petition (Civil) No. 727 of 1995. *Judgment* declared on January 9, 1996.

Supreme Court of India, Committee For C.R. of C.A.P. &Orsvs State Of Arunachal Pradesh &Ors on 17 September, 2015.

Primary sources also include data collected through structured and unstructured interviews with a cross section of the Chakmas. Interviews have been carried out in three districts namely, the Lower Subansiri, the Changlang and the Lohit, where the Chakmas are concentrated. In view of an estimated Chakma population of about 40,000,a stratified random sample of 150 has been proportionately drawn from each of the three districts depending on their population size obtained from village heads. The stratification has been done on the basis of sex, deriving a male and a female from alternate households. Some existing and former General Secretaries, and members of the AAPSU, the DCSU, the CCRCAP, the CRDO, the CWWS, the JAC, the CNCI, the CNCIAP, district officials like Deputy Collectors, Members of the Arunachal Legislative Assembly and the Parliament, NGO leaders, and knowledgeable Chakma leaders have also been interviewed.

Primary data has also been collected from census reports, districts gazetteers, statistical hand books, published and unpublished research works.

Census Reports

Barthakur, J. K., *Census of India, 1971, Series 24, Arunachal Pradesh, General Population Tables,* (New Delhi: Manager Publications, 1973).

Barthakur, J. K., *Census of India, 1971, Series 24, Arunachal Pradesh, Economic Tables,* (Delhi Controller of Publications, n. d.).

Barthakur, J. K., *Census of India, 1971, Series 24, Arunachal Pradesh, Social and Cultural Tables,* (Delhi Controller of Publications, 1972).

Barthakur, J. K., *Census of India, 1971, Series 24, Arunachal Pradesh, Establishment Report, Establishment Table,* (Delhi Controller of Publications, 1972).

Bose, Ashish, *India's Billion Plus People: 2001 Census Highlights, Methodology and Media Coverage,* (Delhi: B. R. Publishing Corporation, 2001), p. 83.

Census of India, 1961, Vol. 24, North-East Frontier Agency, Socio-economic Survey of Jara – A Dafla Village in NEFA, (New Delhi: Manager Publications, 1966).

Census of India: Provisional Population Tables - Census 2011, *censusindia.gov.in.*

International Institute of Population Sciences (Bombay), National Family Health Survey (MCH and Family Planning): *Arunachal Pradesh 1993, Summary Report,* Bombay 1995.

Rai, M. B., *Census of India, 1981, Series 25, Arunachal Pradesh, District Census Handbook, Tirap District, Village and Town Directory, Village and Primary Census Abstract,* (Aligarh: Printwell Printers, n. d.).

Rai, M. B., *Census of India, 1981, Series 25, Arunachal Pradesh, District Census Handbook, Upper Subansiri District, Village Directory, Primary Census Abstract,* (New Delhi Government of India Press, n. d.).

Roy, B. K. and Vijoy S. Verma, *Census of India, 1981, Series 25, Arunachal Pradesh, Regional Divisions of India – A Cartographic Analysis, Occasional Papers; Planning and Supervision,* (n. p. 1988).

Senapati, Tapan, *Census of India, 1991, Series 3, Arunachal Pradesh, Tables on Houses and Household Amenities,* (Delhi Controller of Publications, 1972).

Statistical Pocket Book Arunachal Pradesh, 1985, (Directorate of Economics and Statistics, Government of Arunachal Pradesh, Shillong, 1985).

Thanga, L. B., *Census of India, 1961, Vol. 24, North-East Frontier Agency, General Population Tables and NEFA Special Tables,* (New Delhi: Manager Publications, 1966).

District Gazetteers:

Dutta Choudhury, S., (ed.), *Arunachal Pradesh District Gazetteers: Lohit District,* compiled by Ramendra Narayan Bagchi, (Directorate of Information and Public Relations, Government of Arunachal Pradesh, Shillong, 1978).

Dutta Choudhury, S., (ed.), *Arunachal Pradesh District Gazetteers:Tirap District,* (Directorate of Information and

Public Relations, Government of Arunachal Pradesh, Shillong, 1980).

Dutta Choudhury, S., (ed.), *Arunachal Pradesh District Gazetteers: Subansiri*, compiled by Ramendra Narayan Bagchi, (Directorate of Information and Public Relations, Government of Arunachal Pradesh, Shillong, 1981).

Dutta Choudhury, S., (ed.), *Arunachal Pradesh District Gazetteers: Subansiri*, compiled by Ramendra Narayan Bagchi, (Directorate of Information and Public Relations, Government of Arunachal Pradesh, Shillong, 1981).

Secondary Sources

Encyclopaedias:

Aier, Lima Sasai, (ed.),*Encyclopaedia of Arunachal Pradesh*, Vol. 1 & 2, (New Delhi: Anmol Publications Pvt. Ltd., 2009).

Bareh, H. M., (ed.) *Encyclopaedia of North-East India,* Vol. 1. Arunachal Pradesh, (New Delhi: Mittal Publications, 2001).

Chopra, P. N., (ed.), *Encyclopaedia of India*, Vol. 32. Arunachal Pradesh, by N. S. Olaniya, (New Delhi: Rima Publishing House, 1992-94).

Khanna, S. K., *Encyclopaedia of North-East India: Arunachal Pradesh, Assam, Manipur, Meghalaya, Tripura, Sikkim, Mizoram, Nagaland*, (Delhi: Indian Publishers Distributers, 1994).

Singh, K. S., (ed.), *People of India: Arunachal Pradesh*, Vol. XIV (Calcutta: Seagull Books, 1996).

Shashi, S. S., *Encyclopaedia of Indian Tribes,* Vol. 3. (New Delhi: Anmol Publications, 1994).

The New Encyclopaedia Britannica, Vol. 6, (London: Encyclopeadia Britannica Inc., 1998).

Journal:

Government of Arunachal Pradesh, Research Department, *Resarun*, II, Vol-2, No. 1, Shillong, January, 1976.

Government of Arunachal Pradesh, Research Department, *Resarun*, Spring & Summer Issue, Shillong, 1984.

Books:

Anti Slavery Society, *Chittagong Hill Tracts: Militarization, Oppression and the Hill Tribes,* (London: Anti Slavery Society, 1984).

Baruah, Apurba K., (ed.), *Student Power in North East India: Understanding Student Movements,* (New Delhi: Regency Publication, 2002).

Bhattacharjee, S., *Politics of frontier State: Arunachal Pradesh,* (New Delhi: Omsons Publications, 1994).

Bhattacharyya, Gaytri, *Refugee Rehabilitation and Its Impact on Tripura's Economy*, (New Delhi: Omsons Publications, 1988).

Bose, M. L., *History of Arunachal Pradesh,* (New Delhi: Concept Publishing Company, 1997).

Carter, Marina, *Voices from Indenture: Experiences of Indian Migrants in the British Empire*, (London: Leicester University Press, 1996).

Castles, Stephen and Mark J. Miller, *The Age of Migration: International Population Movements in the Modern World,* (Basingstoke: Palgrave, 2003).

Chakma, Harikishore, et al., *Bara Parang: The Tale of the Development Refugees of the Chittagong Hill Tracts* (Dhaka: Centre for Sustainable Development, 1995).

Chakma, D. K. (ed.), *The Partition and the Chakmas and other writings of Sneha Kumar Chakma*, (Pothi.com, 2013).

Chakraborty, L. N., *Glimpses of the Early History of Arunachal,* (Itanagar: Directorate of Research, Government of Arunachal Pradesh, 1989).

Chittagong Hill Tracts Commission, *Life is Not Ours: Land and Human Rights in the Chittagong Hill Tracts, Bangladesh,'* (Copenhagen, Amsterdam: International Work Group for Indigenous Affairs (IWGIA), Organizing Committee Chittagong Hill Tracts Campaign, May 1991). *Update 1* (1992); *Update 2* (1994); *Update 3* (1997); *Update 4* (2000).

Choudhury, J. N., *Arunachal Panorama: A Study in Profile,* (Shillong: Jaya Choudhury, 1973).

Choudhury, J. N., *Arunachal Pradesh: From Frontier Tracts to Union Territory,* (New Delhi: Cosmo Publications, 1983).

Clark, W. A. V., *Human Migration*, (Beverly Hills: Sage Publications, Inc., 1986).

Cohen, Robin, (ed.), *Theories of Migration*, (Cheltenham and Brookfield: Edward Elger Publishing Company, 1996).

Das, Gurudas, *Tribes of Arunachal Pradesh*, (New Delhi: Vikas Publishing House Pvt. Ltd., 1995).

Das, Gurudas, (ed.) *Research Priorities in North-East India with Special Reference to Arunachal Pradesh,* (New Delhi: Regency Publications, 2001).

Das, N. K., *Ethnic Identity, Ethnicity, and Social Stratification in North-East India,* (New Delhi: Inter-India Publications, 1989).

Dewan, Aditya Kumar, (PhD thesis), *Class and Ethnicity in the Chittagong Hill Tracts of Southeastern Bangladesh*, (submitted in McGill University, 1991).

Datta, P. S., *Economic Development of Arunachal Pradesh: A Case Study of North-Eastern Council's Role,* (New Delhi: Vikas Publishing House Ltd., 1991).

Dutta, S., *Student Movement in Arunachal Pradesh,* (Delhi: Himalayan Publishers, 1998).

Elwin, Verrier, *A Philosophy of NEFA*; with a foreword by Prime Minister of India, 2nd revised edition, Shillong, Advisor to the Government of Assam, 1964.

Elwin, Verrier, *India's North-East Frontier in the Nineteenth Century,* (London: Oxford University Press, 1959).

Esman, Milton Jecob, *Ethnic Politics*, (New York: Cornell University Press, 1994).

Fix, Alan G., *Migration and Colonization in Human Microevolution,* (Cambridge: Cambridge University Press, 1999)

Ferris, Elizabeth G., (ed.), *Refugees and World Politics,* (New York: Praeger Publishers, 1985).

Gassah, L. S., (ed.), *Regional Political Parties in North-East India,* (New Delhi: Omsons Publications, 1992).

Glazer, Nathan, et al., *Beyond the Melting Pot*, (Massachusetts: The M. I. T. Press, 1970).

Ghosh, Subir, *Frontiers Travails – Northeast: The Politics of a Mess*, (New Delhi: Macmillan India Ltd., 2001).

Gopalakrishnan, R., *Ideology, Autonomy and Integration in North-East India: Issues in Political Geography*, (Guwahati: Omsons Publications, 1990).

Grewal, Dalvindar Singh, *Tribes of Arunachal Pradesh: Identity, Culture, and Language*, (Delhi: South Asia Publications, 1997).

Hamilton, A., *In Abhor Jungles of North-East India*, (Indian Edition), (Delhi: Mittal Publications, 1993).

Jha, S. D., *The Wealth of Arunachal Pradesh*, (Delhi: Mittal Publications, 1985).

Jha, S. D., *Arunachal Pradesh: Rich Land and Poor People*, (New Delhi: Omsons Publications, 1986).

Juss, Satvinder S., *Immigration, Nationality and Citizenship*, (London: Mansell, 1993).

Kapoor, M. M., et al., *Educational Administration in Arunachal Pradesh: Structure, Processes and Prospects for the Future*, (New Delhi: Vikas Publishing House Pvt. Ltd., 1994).

Kymlicka, W., *Multicultural Citizenship*, (New York: Oxford University Press, 1995).

Kosinski, A. Leszek and Maudood K. Elahi (eds.), *Population Redistribution and Development in South Asia*, (Dordrecht: D. Reidel Publishing Company, 1985).

Lewis, G. J., *Human Migration: A Geographical Perspective*, (London: Croom Helm, 1982).

Mackenzie, Alexander, *The North-East Frontier of India*, (Delhi: Mittal Publications, 1979).

Mahanta, Prafulla K, *The Tussle between the Citizens and Foreigners in Assam*, (Sahidabad: Vikas Publishing House, 1986).

Michell, John F., *North-East Frontier of India: A Topographical, Political and Military Report*, (Delhi: Vivek Publishing House, 1973).

Mishra, Kamal Kant, *Tribal Elites and Social Transformation,* (New Delhi: Inter-India Publications, 1994).

Mohanta, Bijan, *Administrative Development of Arunachal Pradesh 1875 – 1975,* (New Delhi: Uppal Publishing House, 1984).

Nair, P. Thankappan, *Tribes of Arunachal Pradesh,* (Guwahati: Spectrum Publications, 1985).

Newland, K., *Refugees: The International Politics of Displacement,* (Washington DC: World Watch Institute, 1981).

Osik, N. N., *A Brief History of Arunachal Pradesh,* (New Delhi: Omsons Publication, 1986).

Osik, N. N., *Modern History of Arunachal Pradesh, 1825-1997* (Itanagar: Himalayan Publishers, 1999).

Pakem, B., *Coalition Politics in North-East India,* (New Delhi: Regency Publications, 1999).

Payeng, Habung, *Economic and Social Change in the North-East: A Case Study of Arunachal Pradesh,* (New Delhi: Criterion Publications, 1988).

Safa, H.I. and B.M. Du Toit (eds.), *Migration and Development: Implications for Ethnic Identity and Political Conflict,* (The Hague: Mounton Publishers, 1975).

Shami, Seteney (ed.), *Population, Displacement and Resettlement: Development and Conflict in the Middle East,* (New York: Center for Migration Studies, 1994).

Singh, Chandrika, *Emergence of Arunachal Pradesh as a State,* (Delhi: Mittal Publications, 1989).

Singh, Deepak K, *Stateless in South Asia TheChakmas between Bangladesh and India,* (Delhi: Sage Publications India Pvt. Ltd., 2010).

Sinha, A. C., *Youth Movement in North-East India,* (New Dehli: Har-Anand Publications, 1995).

Talukdar, S. P., *The Chakmas Life and Struggle,* (Delhi: Gian Publishing House, 1988).

Talukdar, Atul Chandra, *Political Transition in the Grass Roots in Tribal India,* (New Delhi: Omsons Publications, 1987).

Weiner, Myron, *Sons of the Soil: Migration and Ethnic Conflict in India*, (Delhi: Oxford University Press, 1978).

Weiner, Myron, *When Migrants Succeed and Natives fail: Assam and its Migrants*, (Cambridge: M.I.T. Center for International Studies Working Paper, February, 1975).

Weiner, Myron and Michael S. Teitelbaum, *Political Demography, Democratic Engineering,* (New York: Berghahn Books, 2001), p. ix.

Van Ham, Peter and AglajaStirn, *The Seven Sisters of India: Tribal Worlds between Tibet and Burma,* (Ahmedabad: Mapin Publishing Pvt. Ltd., 2000).

Van Hear, Nicholas, *New Diasporas: The mass exodus, dispersal and regrouping of migrant communities*, (London: UCL Press, 1998).

Van Schendel, Willem, et al., *The Chittagong Hill Tracts: Living in a Borderland*, (Bangkok: White Lotus, 2000).

Woods, R., *Theoretical Population Geography*, (London and New York: Longman, 1982).

Zimmermann, Klaus F., (ed.), *Migration and Economic Development*, (Heidelberg: Springer-Verlag, 1992).

Zolberg, Aristide R., *Escape from Violence: the Refugee Crisis in the Developing World*, (Oxford: Oxford University Press, 1989).

Articles in Books

Dutta, S., "Chakma-Hajong Refugee Problem in Arunachal Pradesh: A Historical Background," *Proceedings of the North East History Association* (Department of History, North-Eastern Hill University, Shillong), No. 16. (1995), 333-338.

Dutta, S., "Student Movement in Arunachal Pradesh", in A. K. Baruah (ed.), *Student Power in North-East India: Understanding Student Movements,* (New Delhi: Regency Publication, 2002), pp.197-231.

George de Vos, "Ethnic Pluralism," in George de Vos and Lola Romanucci-Ross (eds.), *Ethnic Identity: Cultural Continuities and Change,* (California: Mayfield Publishing Co., 1975), pp. 15-25.

Mabogunje, Akin L., 'Systems Approach to a Theory of Rural-Urban Migration,' in Robin Cohen (ed.), *Theories of Migration,* (Cheltenham: Edward Elgar Publishing Ltd., 1996), pp. 44-58.

Phadnis, Urmila, "Ethnic Groups in the Politics of Sri Lanka," in David Taylor and Malcolm Yapp (eds.), Political Identity in South Asia, (London: Curzon Press, 1979), pp. 191-242.

Sen Gupta, Susmita, "Ethnic Issues and All Arunachal Students' Union", *Proceedings of the North East India Political Science Association,* Seventh Annual Conference, (North-Eastern Hill University, Tura Campus, December, 1997), pp. 39-47.

Sen Gupta, Susmita, "Migration and Politics in Arunachal Pradesh – Some Observation," *Proceedings of the North East India Political Science Association,* 10th Annual Conference, (Gauhati University, Gauhati, December 21-23, 2000), pp. 92-101.

Talukdar, A. C., "Political Evolution of Arunachal Pradesh", *Proceedings of the North East History Association* (Department of History, North-Eastern Hill University, Shillong), No. 7. (1986), pp. 131-136.

Talukdar, A. C., "Regional Political Party in Arunachal Pradesh-Its Nature and Role in State Politics," in B. Pakem (ed.), *Regionalism in India, with special reference to North East India,* (New Delhi: Har-Anand Publications, 1993), pp. 289-301.

Weiner, Myron, 'Rejected Peoples and Unwanted Migrants in South Asia', in *Economic and Political Weekly*, Vol. 28, No. 34, Mumbai, August 21, 1993, pp. 1737-1746.

Zolberg, Aristide R., 'The Formation of New States as a Refugee-Generating Process,' in Robin Cohen (ed.), *Theories of Migration,* (Cheltenham: Edward Elgar Publishing Ltd., 1996), pp. 282-296.

Newspaper Reports:

Amit Anand Choudhury, "Grant citizenship to Chakma refugees within 3 months: Supreme Court," *The Times of India*, New Delhi, September 18, 2015, p. 1.

Banerjee, Ruben, "Chakmas Living under the Notice of Death," *India Today,* October 15, 1994, pp. 42-43.

Bhakti, Kumar, "Strong resentment over Jacob's statement, Chakmas are citizens of Arunachal," *The Echo of Arunachal*, December 9-15, 1992.

Chakma, S. K., "Chakma Refugees," *The Telescope,*Agartala, June 18, 1975, pp. 1-2.

Chakrabarti, Ashis, "Arunachal CM sets deadline on refugee deportation," *The Indian Express,* New Delhi, December 8, 1995, p. 19.

Choudhury, Rabijit, "Arunachal Chakmas Struggle for their rights," *The Statesman,* September 29, 1994, p. 16.

Das, Ripunjoy, "AAPSU critical of centre's stand on Chakma refugees," *The Assam Tribune*, Guwahati, December 4, 1992, p. 1.

Datta, Sekhar, "Rootless, after a 28-yr struggle," *The Telegraph*, Calcutta, October 17, 1992, p.11.

Sen, Dev, Antara and Samudra Gupta Kashyap, "Paperless People," *The Indian Express,* New Delhi, October 9, 1994, 5-6.

Gilani, Iftikhar, "Chakma Refugees: The Spectre of Deportation," *The Nation and the World*, New Delhi, December 1, 1992, pp. 16-17.

Hazarika, Sanjoy, "Chakmas' flight to nowhere," *The Indian Express,* New Delhi, October 17, 1994.

Hussain, Wasbir, "Chakma allege state terrorism in Arunachal," *The Asian Age,* Calcutta, May 31, 1995, p. 5.

Hussain, Wasbir, "Chakmas threaten stir over issue of citizenship," *The Asian Age,* Calcutta, June 21, 1995, p. 5.

Lama, J. B., "Chakma Refugees", *The Statesman*, New Delhi, April 15, 2002, p. 7.

Rao, T. Padmanabha, "SC asks Arunachal to protect Chakmas," *The Hindu,* New Delhi, January 11, 1996, p. 12.

Sharma, Rajnish, "EC Threatens not to hold poll in Chakma areas," *The Hindustan Times,* New Delhi, February 26, 2004, p. 8.

"Amnesty urges Rao to protect Chakmas," *The Statesman,* New Delhi, November 1, 1994.

"Arunachal to Press Centre for Shifting of Chakma, Hojong Refugees," *The Shillong Times*, Shillong, October 29, 1993. P. 3.

"Assam curfew on borders," *The Hindustan Times,* New Delhi, September 15, 1994, p. 24.

"Chakma Issue to be Raised during Advani's Arunachal Trip," *The Shillong Times*, Shillong, October 31, 1993, p. 3.

"Chakmas are Citizens of Arunachal," *The Echo of Arunachal*, Naharlagun, December 9-15, 1992.

"Chakmas clash with students, 5 injured," *The Telegraph*, Guwahati, August 11, 2010, p. 17.

"Chakmas threaten stir over the issue of citizenship," *The Asian Age*, Calcutta, June 21, 1995.

"Chakmas, Hajongs reject relocation move, demand permanent solution to refugee issue," *The Arunachal Times*, Itanagar, August 25, 2021, p. 1.

"Discrimination against Chakmas in Arunachal," *The Meghalaya Guardian*, Shillong, November 27, 1992.

"Fear grips Arunachal on eve of AAPSU deadline," *The Statesman,* Calcutta, September 30, 1994.

"Government reiterates demand for immediate deportation," *The Sentinel*, Guwahati, September 26, 1993, p. 2.

"House okays Chakma deportation move," *The Arunachal Times*, Naharlagun, December 4, 1992.

"JAC urges MHA to resolve Chakma-Hajong issue; seeks autonomous council if not assimilation," *The Arunachal Times*, Itanagar, February 22, 2022, p. 1.

"Khandu moves poll panel after violence," *The Telegraph*, Guwahati, August 12, 2010, p. 17.

"NHRC directs MHA to protect rights of Arunachal Chakmas," *The Hindu*, Guwahati, January 25, 2022, p. 7.

"No citizenship in near future," *The Sentinel*, Guwahati, November 11, 1992.

"Proper plan needed for Chakma-Hajong relocation," *The Arunachal Times*, Itanagar, August 26, 2021, p. 1.

"Saikia refutes Apang's charge on Chakma influx," *The Pioneer,* New Delhi, September, 1994, p. 4.

"Solution to Chakma issue likely," *The Hindustan Times*, New Delhi, June 21, 1995.

"Students' body welcomes Arunachal Pradesh move to relocate Chakmas, Hajongs," *The Hindu*, Guwahati, August 26, 2021, p. 6.

"Students' union files PIL against Chakmas." *The Telegraph, Guwahati,* June 11, 2009, p. 16.

APPENDICES

APPENDIX - I

IN THE SUPREME COURT OF INDIA ORIGINAL CIVIL JURISDICTION WRIT PETITION (CIVIL) NO. 720 OF 1995

National Human Rights Commission . . . Petitioner

Versus

State of Arunachal Pradesh & Anr. . . . Respondents

JUDGMENT

AHMADI, CJI

This public interest petition, being a writ petition under Article 32 of the Constitution, has been filed by the National Human Rights Commission (hereinafter called "NHRC") and seeks to enforce the rights, under Article 21 of the Constitution, of about 65,000 Chakma/ Hajong tribals (hereafter called 'Chakmas"). It is alleged that these Chakmas, settled mainly in the State of Arunachal Pradesh, are being persecuted by sections of the citizens of Arunachal Pradesh. The first respondent is the State of Arunachal Pradesh and the second respondent is the Union of India.

The NHRC has been set up under the protection or Human Rights Act, 1993 (No. 10 of 1994). Section 18 of this Act empowers the NHRC to approach this Court in appropriate cases.

The factual matrix of the case may now be referred to. A large number of Chakmas from erstwhile East

Pakistan (now Bangladesh) were displaced by the Kaptai Hydel Power Project in 1954. They had taken shelter in Assam and Tripura. Most of them were settled in these States and became Indian citizens in due course of time. Since a large number of refugees had taken shelter in Assam, the State Government had expressed its inability to rehabilitate all of them and requested assistance in this regard from certain other States. Thereafter, in consultation with the erstwhile NEFA administration (North East Frontier Agency - Arunachal Pradesh), about 4,012 Chakma families were settled in parts of NEFA. They were also allotted some land in consultation with local tribals. The Government of India had also sanctioned rehabilitation assistance @ Rs. 4,200/- per family. The present population of Chakmas in Arunachal Pradesh in estimated to be around 65,000.

The issue of conferring citizenship on the Chakmas was considered by the second respondent from time to time. The Minister of State for Home Affairs has on several occasions expressed the intention of the second respondent in this regard. Groups of Chakmas have represented to the petitioner that they have made representations for the grant of citizenship under Section 5(1)(a) of the Citizenship Act, 1995 (hereinafter called "The Act") before their local Deputy Commissioners but no decision has been communicated to them. In recent years, relations between citizens of Arunachal Pradesh and the Chakmas have deteriorated, and the latter have complained that they are being subjected to repressive measures with a view to forcibly expelling them from the State of Arunachal Pradesh.

On September 9, 1994, the People's Union for Civil Liberties, Delhi brought this issue to the attention of the NHRC which issued letters to the Chief Secretary, Arunachal Pradesh and the Home Secretary, Government' of India making enquiries in this regard.

On September 30, 1994, the Chief Secretary of Arunachal Pradesh faxed a reply stating that the situation was totally under control and adequate police protection had been given to the Chakmas.

On October 15, 1994, the Committee for Citizenship Rights of the Chakmas (hereinafter called "The CCRC") filed a representation with the NHRC complaining of the persecution of the Chakmas. The petition contained a press report carried in "The Telegraph" dated August 26, 1994 stating that the All Arunachal Pradesh Students Union (hereinafter called "AAPSU") has issued "quit notices" to all alleged foreigners, including the Chakmas, to leave the State by September 30, 1995. The AAPSU had threatened to use force if its demand was not acceded to. The matter was treated as a formal complaint by the NHRC and on October 28, 1994, it issued notices to the first and the second respondents calling for their reports on the issue.

On November 22, 1994, the Ministry of Home Affairs sent a note to the petitioner reaffirming its intention of granting citizenship to the Chakmas. It also pointed out that Central Reserve Forces had been deployed in response to the threat of the AAPSU and that the State Administration had been directed to ensure the protection of the Chakmas. On December 7, 1994, the NHRC directed that first and second respondents to appraise it of the steps taken to protect the Chakmas. This direction was ignored till September, 1995 despite the sending of reminders. On September 25, 1995, the first respondent filed an interim reply and asked for time of four weeks' duration to file a supplementary report. The first respondent did not, however, comply with its own deadline.

On October 12, 1995 and again on October 28, 1995 the CCRC sent urgent petitions to the NHRC alleging immediate threats to the lives of the Chakmas. On October 29, 1995, the NHRC recorded a prima facie conclusion that the officers of the first respondent were acting in coordination with the AAPSU with a view to expelling the Chakmas from the State of Arunachal Pradesh. The NHRC stated that since the first respondent was delaying the matter, and since it had doubts as to whether its own efforts would be sufficient to sustain the Chakmas in their own habitat, it had decided to approach this Court to seek appropriate reliefs.

On November 2, 1995, this Court issued an interim order directing the first respondent to ensure that the Chakmas situated in its territory are not ousted by any coercive action, not in accordance with law.

We may now refer to the stance of the Union of India, the second respondent, on the issue. It has been pointed out that, in 1964, pursuant to extensive discussions between the Government of India and the NEFA administration, it was decided to sent the Chakmas for the purpose of their resettlement to the territory of the Arunachal Pradesh for more than three decades, having developed close social, religious and economic ties. To uproot them at this stage would be both impracticable and inhuman. Our attention has been drawn to a Joint Statement issued by the Prime Ministers of India and Bangladesh at New Delhi in February 1972, pursuant to which the Union Government had conveyed to all the States concerned, it's decision to confer citizenship on the Chakmas, in accordance with Section 5(1)(a) of the Act. The second respondent further states that the children of the Chakmas, who were born in India prior to he amendment of the Act in 1987, would have legitimate claims to citizenship. According to the Union of India, the first respondent has been expressing reservations on this account. By not forwarding the applications submitted by the Chakmas along with their reports for grant of citizenship as required by Rule 9 of the Citizenship Rules, 1995, the officers of the first respondent are preventing the Union of India from considering the issue of citizenship of the Chakmas. We are further informed that the Union of India is actively considering the issue of citizenship and has recommended to the first respondent that it take all necessary steps for providing security to the Chakmas. To this end, central para-military forces have been made available for deployment in the strife-ridden areas. The Union Government favours a dialogue, between the State Government, the Chakmas and all concerned within the State to amicably resolve the issue of granting citizenship to the Chakmas while also redressing the genuine grievances of the citizens of Arunachal Pradesh.

The first respondent, in its counter to the petition, has contended before us that the allegation of violation of human rights are incorrect, that it has taken bona fide and sincere steps towards providing the Chakmas with basic amenities and has, to the best of its ability, protected their lives and properties. It is further contended that the issue of citizenship of the Chakmas has been conclusively determined by the decision of this Court in State of Arunachal Pradesh vs. Khudiram Chakma (1994 Supp. (1) SCC 615 - hereinafter called "Khudiram Chakma's case"). It is therefore contended that since the Chakmas are foreigners, they are not entitled to the protection of fundamental rights except Article 21. This being so, the authorities may, at any time, ask the Chakmas to quit the state, if they so desire. According to the first respondent, having lost their case in this Court, the Chakmas have "raised a bogey of violation of human rights."

The first respondent has filed a counter to the stand taken by the Union of India. The first respondent denies that the Union of India had sent the CRPF Battalions of its own accord; according to it, they were sent pursuant to its letter dated 20.9.1994 asking for assistance. It has also denied that certain Chakmas were killed on account of economic blockades effected by the AAPSU; according to it, these casualties were the result of a malarial epidemic. The first respondent reiterates that the sui generis Constitutional position of the State debars it from permitting outsiders to the settled within its territory, that it has limited resources and that its economy is mainly dependent on the vagaries of nature; and that it has no financial resources to tend to the needs of the Chakmas having already spent approximately Rs.100 crores on their upkeep. It has also been stated that the Union of India has refused to share its financial responsibility for the upkeep of the Chakmas.

Referring to the issue of grant of citizenship it is submitted as follows:

> "It is submitted that under the Citizenship Act, 1995 and the Rules made thereunder a specific procedure is provided for grant of citizenship. According to that after receiving the application, the DC of the area makes necessary enquiries about the antecedents of the applicant and after getting a satisfactory report forwards the case to the State Government which in turn forwards it to the Central Government. It is submitted that on enquiry if the report is adverse the DC would not forward it further. It is submitted that the applications, if any, made in this regard have already been disposed of after necessary enquiry. There is no application pending before the DC."

It may be pointed out that this stand of the first respondent is in direct contravention of the stand adopted by it in the representation dated September 25, 1995, submitted by it to the NHRC where it had stated:

> "The question of grant of citizenship is entirely governed by the Citizenship Act, 1995 and the Central Government is the sole authority to grant citizenship. The State Government has no jurisdiction in the matter."

It is further submitted by the first respondent that under the Constitution, the State of Arunachal Pradesh enjoys a special status and, bearing in mind its ethnicity, it has been declared that it would be administered under Part X of the Constitution. That is the reason why laws and regulations applicable during the British Regime continue to apply even today. The settlement of Chakmas in large numbers in the State would disturb its ethnic balance and destroy its culture and identity. The special provisions made in the Construction would be set at naught if the State's tribal population is allowed to be invaded by people from outside. The tribals, therefore, consider Chakmas as a potential threat to their tradition and culture and are, therefore, keen that the latter do not entrench themselves in the State. Besides, the financial resources of the State without Central assistance, which is ordinarily not forthcoming, would throw a heavy burden on the State which it would find well nigh impossible to bear. In the circumstances, contends the first respondent, it is unfair and unconstitutional to throw the burden of such a large number of Chakmas on the State.

We are unable to accept the contention of the first respondent that no threat exists to the life and liberty of the Chakmas guarantee by Article 21 of the Constitution, and that it has taken adequate steps to ensure the protection of the Chakmas. After handling the present matter for more than a year, the NHRC recorded a prima facie finding that the service of quit notices and their admitted enforcement appeared to be supported by the officers of the first respondent. The NHRC further held that the first respondent had, on the one hand, delayed the disposal of the matter by not furnishing the required response and had, on the other hand, sought to enforce the eviction of the Chakmas through its agencies. It is to be noted that, at no time, has the first respondent sought to condemn the activities of the AAPSU. However, the most damning facts against the first respondent are to be found in the counter affidavit of the second respondent. In the assessment of the Union of India, the threat posed by the AAPSU was grave enough to warrant the placing of two additional battalions of CRPF at the disposal of the State Administration. Whether it was done at the behest of the State Government or by the Union on its own is of no consequence; the fact that it had become necessary speaks for itself. The second respondent further notes that after the expiry of the deadline of October 30, 1994, the AAPSU and other tribal student organisations continued to agitate and press for the expulsion of all foreigners including the Chakmas. It was reported that the AAPSU had started enforcing of economic blockades on the refugee camps, which adversely affected the supply of rations, medical and essential facilities etc. to the Chakmas. Of course the State Government has denied the allegation, but the independent inquiry of the NHRC shows otherwise. The fact that the Chakmas were dying on account of the blockade for want of medicines is an established fact. After reports regarding lack of medical facilities and the spread of malaria and dysentery in Chakma settlements were received, the Union Government advised the first respondent to ensure normal supplies of essential commodities to the Chakma settlement. On September 20, 1995, the AAPSU once again issued an ultimatum citing December 31, 1995 as the fresh deadline for the ousting of Chakmas. This is yet another threat which the first respondent has not indicated how it proposes to counter.

It is, therefore, clear that there exists a clear and present danger to the lives and personal liberty of the Chakmas. In Louis De Raedt v. Union of India [(1991) 3 SCC 554] and Khudiram Chakma's case this court held that foreigners are entitled to the protection of Article of Article 21 of the Constitution.

The contention of the first respondent that the ruling of this Court in Khudiram Chakma's case has for closed the consideration of the citizenship of Chakmas is misconceived. The facts of that case reveal that the appellant and 56 families migrated to India in 1964 from erstwhile East Pakistan and were lodged in the Government Refugee Camp at Ledo. They were later shifted to another camp at Miao. In 1996, the State Government drew up the Chakma Resettlement Scheme for refugees and the Chakmas were allotted lands in two villages. The appellant, however, stayed out and secured land in another area by private negotiations. The State questioned the legality of the said transaction since, under the Regulations then in force, no person other than a native of that District could acquire land in it. Since there were complaints against the appellant and others who had settled on this land, the State by order dated February 15, 1984, directed that they shift to the area earmarked for them. This order was challenged on the ground that Chakmas who had settled there were citizens of India and by seeking their forcible eviction, the State was violating their fundamental rights and, in any case, the order was arbitrary and illegal as violative of the principles of natural justice. On the question of citizenship, they invoked section 6-A of the Act which, inter alia, provides that all persons of Indian origin who came before January 1, 1996 to Assam from territories included in Bangladesh immediately before the commencement of the Citizenship (Amendment) Act, 1985, and who had been ordinarily resident in Assam since their entry into Assam shall be deemed to be citizens of India as from January 1, 1996. Others who had come to Assam after that date and before March 25, 1971, and had been ordinarily resident in Assam since then and had been detected to be foreigners, could register themselves. It will thus be seen that the appellant and others claimed citizenship under this special provision made pursuant to the Assam Accord. The High Court held that the appellant and others did not fall under the said category as they had stayed in Assam for a short period in 1964 and had strayed away therefrom in the area now within the State of Arunachal Pradesh. On appeal, this court affirmed that view. It is, therefore, clear that in that case, the Court was required to consider the claim of citizenship based on the language of Section 6-A of the Act. Thus, in Khudiram Chakma's case, this Court was seized of a matter where 57 Chakma families were seeking to challenge an order requiring them to vacate land bought by them in direct contravention of clause 7 of the Bengal Eastern Frontier Regulation, 1873. The issue of citizenship was raised in a narrower context and was limited to Section 6-A (2) of the Act. The Court observed that the Chakmas in that case, who were resident in Arunachal Pradesh, could not avail of the benefit of Section 6A of the Act which is a special provision for the citizenship of persons covered by the Assam Accord. In the present case, the Chakmas are seeking to obtain citizenship under Section 5(1)(a) of the Act, where the consideration are entirely different. That Section provides for citizenship by registration. It says that the prescribed authority may, on receipt of an application in that behalf, register a person who is not a citizen of India, as a citizen of India if he/she satisfies the conditions set out therein. This provision is of general application and is not limited to persons belonging to a certain group only as in the case of Section 6-A. Section 5, therefore, can be invoked by persons who are not citizens of India but are seeking citizenship by registration. Such applications would have to be in the form prescribed by part II of the Citizenship Rules, 1956 (hereinafter called "The Rules"). Under Rule 7, such application has to be made to the Collector within whose jurisdiction the applicant is ordinarily resident. Rule 8 describes the authority to register a person as a citizen of India under Section 5(1) of the Act. It says that the authority to register a person as a citizen of India shall be an officer not below the rank of a Deputy Secretary to the Government of India in the Ministry of Home Affairs, and also includes such officer as the Central Government may, by a notification in the Official Gazette, appoint and in any other cases falling under the Rules, any officer not below the rank of a Joint Secretary to the Government of India in the Ministry of Home Affairs, and also includes such other officer as the Central Government may, by notification in the official Gazette, appoint. Rule 9 next enjoins the Collector to transmit every application received by him under Section 5 (1) (a) to the Central Government through the State Government or the Union Territory administration, as the case may be, along with a report on matters set out in clauses (a) to (e) thereof. Rule 10 provides for issuance of a certificate to be granted to persons registered as citizens and Rules 11 and 12 provide for maintenance of registers. These are the relevant rules in regard to registration of persons as citizens of India.

From what we have said hereinbefore, there is no doubt that the Chakmas who migrated from East-Pakistan (now Bangladesh) in 1964, first settled down in the State of Assam and then shifted to areas which now fall within the State of Arunachal Pradesh. They have settled there since the last about two and a half decades and have raised their families in the said State. Their children have married and they too have had children. Thus, a large number of them were born in the State itself. Now it is proposed to uproot them by force. The AAPSU has been giving out threats to forcibly drive them out to the neighbouring State which in turn is unwilling to accept them. The residents of the neighbouring State have also threatened to kill them if they try to enter their State. They are thus sandwiched between two forces, each pushing in opposite direction which can only hurt them. Faced with the prospect of annihilation the NHRC was moved, which finding it impossible to extend protection to them, moved this Court for certain reliefs.

By virtue of their long and prolonged stay in the State, the Chakmas who migrated to, and those born in the State, seek citizenship under the Constitution read with Section 5 of the Act. We have already indicated earlier that if a person satisfies the requirements of Section 5 of the Act, he/she can be registered as a citizen of India. The procedure to be followed in processing such requests has been outlined in Part II of the Rules. We have adverted to the relevant rules hereinbefore. According to these rules, the application for registration has to be made in the prescribed form, duly affirmed, to the Collector within whose jurisdiction he resides. After the application is so received, the authority to register a person as a citizen of India, is vested in the officer named under Rule 8 of the Rules. Under Rule 9, the Collector is expected to transmit every application under Section 5(1)(a) of the Acts to the Central Government. On a conjoint reading of Rules 8 and 9 it becomes clear that the Collector has merely to receive the application and forward it to the Central Government. It is only the authority constituted under Rule 8 which is empowered to register a person as a citizen of India. It follows that only that authority can refuse to entertain an application made under Section 5 of the Act. Yet it is an admitted fact that after receipt of the application, the Deputy Collector (DC) makes an enquiry and if the report it adverse, the DC refuses to forward the application; in other words, he rejects the application at the threshold and does not forward it to the Central Government. The grievance of the Central Government is that since the DC does not forward it to the Central Government. The grievance of the Central Government is that since the DC does not forward the applications, it is not in a position to take a decision whether or not to register the person as a citizen of India. That is why it is said that the DC or Collector, who receives the application should be directed to forward the same to the Central Government to enable it to decide the request on merits. It is obvious that by refusing to forward the applications of the Chakmas to the Central Government, the DC is failing in his duty and is also preventing the Central Government from performing its duty under the Act and the Rules.

We are a country governed by the Rule of Law. Our Constitution confers certain rights on every human being and certain other rights on citizens. Every person is entitled to equality before the law and equal protection of the laws. So also, no person can be deprived of his life or personal liberty except according to procedure established by law. Thus the State is bound to protect the life and liberty of every human-being, be he a citizen or otherwise, and it cannot permit anybody or group of persons, e.g., the AAPSU, to threaten the Chakmas to leave the State, failing which they would be forced to do so. No State Government worth the name can tolerate such threats by one group of persons to another group of persons; it is duty bound to protect. The threatened group from such assaults and if it fails to do so, it will fail to perform its Constitutional as well as statutory obligations. Those giving such threats would be liable to be dealt with in accordance with law. The State Government must act impartially and carry out its legal obligations. Those giving such threats would be liable to be dealt with in accordance with law. The State Government must act impartially and carry out its legal obligations to safeguard the life, health and well-being of Chakmas residing in the State without being inhibited by local politics. Besides, by refusing to forward their applications, the Chakmas are denied rights, Constitutional and statutory to be considered for being registered as citizens of India.

In view of the above, we allow this petition and direct the first and second respondents, by way of a writ of mandamus, as under:-

(1) The first respondent, the State of Arunachal Pradesh, shall ensure that the life and personal liberty of each and every Chakma residing within the State shall be protected and any attempt to forcibly evict or drive them out of the State by organised groups, such as the AAPSU, shall be repelled, if necessary by requisitioning the service of para-military or police force, and if additional forces are considered necessary to carry out this direction, the first respondent will request the second respondent, the Union of India, to provide such additional force, and the second respondent shall provide such additional force as is necessary to protect the lives and liberty of the Chakmas;

(2) Except in accordance with law, the Chakmas shall not be evicted from their homes and shall not be denied domestic life and comfort therein;

(3) The quit notices and ultimatums issued by the AAPSU and any other group which tantamount to threats to the life and liberty of each and every Chakma should be dealt with by the first respondent in accordance with law;

(4) The application made for registration as citizen of India by the Chakma or Chakmas under Section 5 of the Act, shall be entered in the register maintained for the purpose and shall be forwarded by the Collector or the DC who receives them under the relevant rule, with or without enquiry, as the case may be, to the Central Government for its consideration in accordance with law; even returned applications shall be called back or fresh ones shall be obtained from the concerned persons and shall be processed and forwarded to the Central Government;

(5) While the application of any individual Chakma is pending consideration, the first respondent shall not evict or remove the concerned person from his occupation on the ground that he is not a citizen of India until the competent authority has taken a decision in that behalf; and (6) the first respondent will pay to the petitioner cost of this petition which we quantity at Rs.10, 000/- within six weeks from today by depositing the same in the office of the NHRC, New Delhi.

The petition shall stand so disposed of.

.... CJI
.... J.
(S. C. Sen)
New Delhi
January 9, 1996.

APPENDIX - II

ELECTION COMMISSION OF INDIA

Nirvachan Sadan, Ashoka Road, New Delhi

No. 23/ARUN/2003

Dated: 3rd March, 2004

O R D E R

The Government of India, during the period 1964-69, settled some Chakma refugees from Bangladesh in Arunachal Pradesh. Their population has increased manifold. The Committee for Citizenship Rights of the Chakmas has been demanding conferment of Indian citizenship status and enrolment of their names in the electoral rolls. The said Committee has taken the matter to the National Human Rights Commission and the Supreme Court of India. The Hon'ble Supreme Court vide order dated 09-01-1996 directed the Government of India and the State Government of Arunachal Pradesh to settle the issue expeditiously and further directed, inter alia, that the State Government shall ensure that the life and personal liberty of each and every Chakma residing within the State of Arunachal Pradesh shall be protected and any attempt to forcibly evict or drive them out of the State by any organized group shall be repelled. In the meanwhile, the High Court of Delhi vide order dated 28-09-2000 held that such of the Chakmas who were born in India after their settlement in the State of Arunachal Pradesh but before 01-07-1987, became citizens of India by birth under section 3(1) (a) of the Citizenship Act even if their parents were not citizens of India at the time of their birth.

The Election Commission is concerned with the enrolment as electors of those Chakmas who have acquired Indian citizenship by birth as aforesaid and who are ordinarily resident in Arunachal Pradesh. Under the provisions of Article 326 of the Constitution read with section 19 of the Representation of the People Act, 1950, these Chakmas are constitutionally entitled to be registered as electors in the electoral rolls of the constituencies in which they are ordinarily resident in Arunachal Pradesh. These constituencies are 14-Doimukh (ST), 46-Chowkham (ST), 49-Bordumsa Diyum and 50-Miao (ST) assembly constituencies.

The Commission vide its orders dated 31st March, 2003 and 24th April, 2003 ordered a special summary revision of electoral rolls in Arunachal Pradesh with reference to 01-01-2003 as the qualifying date in the above-mentioned Assembly Constituencies. During the process of the said summary revision of electoral rolls, the concerned Electoral Registration Officers of the above said assembly constituencies accepted 323, 1164 and 10 claims of the Chakmas for inclusion in the electoral rolls of 46-Chowkham (ST), 49-Bordumsa Diyum and 50-Miao (ST) assembly constituencies respectively after due process. The Electoral Registration Officer of 14-Doimukh (ST) Assembly Constituency reported that he had rejected all the 426 applications for inclusion of names received by him by post from the Chakmas on the ground that those applications were received in bulk. Unfortunately, subsequently, the State Cabinet passed a resolution dated 14-05-2003, which directed that non Arunachaleese shall not be entitled to be enrolled in the electoral rolls in the State unless they possessed Inner Line Permits under the Bengal East Area and Frontier Regulation, 1873, having a minimum validity period of six months. Apparently influenced by the above said resolution of the State cabinet, the concerned Electoral Registration Officers rejected the said accepted claims. In view of the above, the Commission vide its d.o.letter dated 10-09-2003 addressed to the State Chief Minister brought it to his notice, inter-alia that the preparation and revision of electoral rolls was a constitutional duty conferred on the Commission by Article 324 (1) of the Constitution and the preparation and revision of electoral rolls were governed by the provisions of the Constitution and the Acts and the rules relating thereto and that the State cabinet resolution dated 14-05-2003 in so far as it related to the preparation and revision of electoral rolls was not in consonance with the provisions of the constitution and acts and rules governing the matter. The Commission also instructed the Chief Electoral Officer, Arunachal Pradesh to direct the Electoral Registration Officers of the above said three assembly constituencies to revive their earlier decisions to include the names of Chakmas who were found to be eligible, in the relevant electoral rolls. The State Chief Electoral Officer informed the Commission that the Electoral registration Officers of the said three assembly constituencies did not follow the Commission's instructions asking them to revive their earlier decisions to include the names of Chakmas found to be eligible, in the relevant electoral roll. The Chief Electoral Officer also reported that the Electoral Registration of 14-Doimukh (ST) Assembly Constituency had reported that he had not received any applications for inclusion of names. But actually this report was not correct as it was earlier reported that he had received 426 applications for inclusion and these were rejected by him on the ground that these were received in bulk. In these compelling circumstances, the Commission, by its order dated 02-01-2004 declared that it shall not conduct any elections or carry out any election related work, including preparation and revision of electoral rolls, in these four assembly constituencies unless the State Cabinet withdrew or amended appropriately its resolution dated 14.05.2003 and created conditions conducive for the preparation and revision of accurate and defect-free electoral rolls as per the provisions of the Constitution and of the Acts and Rules governing the matter in these four Assembly Constituencies.

In the context of the forthcoming general election to the Lok Sabha, the Commission has reviewed the entire matter and took note of the fact that suspension of election related work as ordered by the Commission by its order dated 2nd January, 2004, in the above mentioned four Assembly Constituencies which spread over both the Parliamentary Constituencies in the State, would consequently deprive the entire electorate of the State of the opportunity to elect their representatives to the House of the People in the forthcoming general elections to the Lok Sabha along with other States.

Under Article 325 of the Constitution, it is laid down that no person shall be ineligible for inclusion in or claim to be included in any electoral roll for any constituency on grounds only of religion, race, castes, sex or any of them. It is evident that the names of the aforesaid eligible Chakmas in the State of Arunachal Pradesh have not been included in the electoral rolls mainly for the reason that they belong to the Chakma tribe/race, which is violative of the Constitutional mandate of Article 325.

Having regard to the above facts and circumstances the Election Commission, in exercise of its plenary powers conferred on it by Article 324 of the Constitution and in supersession of its order No. 23/Arun-AL/2003 dated 2.1.2004, hereby orders and directs that the names of 323, 1164 and 10 Chakmas of 46-Chowkham (ST), 49-Bordumsa Diyum and 50-Miao (ST) Assembly Constituencies respectively who were found to be eligible for inclusion in the respective electoral rolls by the concerned Electoral Registration Officers during the special summary revision of electoral rolls w.r.t. 1.1.2003 as qualifying date, ordered by the Commission vide its orders dated 31st March, 2003 and 24th April, 2003 and prior to the resolution dated 14-05-2003 of the State cabinet, shall be deemed to have been included in the electoral rolls of the respective Assembly Constituencies by virtue of the provisions of Articles 325 and 326 of the Constitution and Section 19 of the Representation of the People Act, 1950 . A complete list of the names of the said 1497 eligible electors is given in Annexure-I hereto. The Electoral registration Officers of the above mentioned three Assembly Constituencies shall forthwith publish the electoral rolls by including the names of the aforesaid 1497 eligible electors in the relevant parts of the electoral rolls of the respective Assembly Constituencies and they shall be eligible to cast their votes under Section 62 of the Representation of the People Act, 1951 in the ensuing elections to the House of the People. The Electoral Registration Officer for 14-Doimukh Assembly Constituency shall also publish the electoral rolls as finalized by him, forthwith.

(N. GOPALASWAMI)
ELECTION COMMISSIONER

(B.B. TANDON)
ELECTION COMMISSIONER

(T.S. KRISHNAMURTHY)
CHIEF ELECTION COMMISSIONER

APPENDIX - III

SUPREME COURT OF INDIA

Committee for C.R. of C.A.P. &Orsvs State of Arunachal Pradesh &Ors on 17 September, 2015

Author: ....J.

Bench: Anil R. Dave, Adarsh Kumar Goel

REPORTABLE

IN THE SUPREME COURT OF INDIA

CIVIL ORIGINAL JURISDICTION

WRIT PETITION (CIVIL) NO.510 OF 2007

COMMITTEE FOR C.R. OF C.A.P. & ORS. ...PETITIONERS

VERSUS

STATE OF ARUNACHAL PRADESH & ORS. ...RESPONDENTS

J U D G M E N T

ADARSH KUMAR GOEL, J.

1. This petition under Article 32 of the Constitution of India mainly seeks direction against Union of India through Ministry of Home Affairs to grant citizenship to the Chakma and HajongTribals who migrated to India in 1964-1969 and were settled in the State of Arunachal Pradesh.

2. Petitioner No.1 has described itself as "Committee for Citizenship Rights of the Chakmas of Arunachal Pradesh" ("CCRC"). According to the averments in the petition, representations were filed with the National Human Rights Commission ("NHRC") alleging persecution of Chakmas and Hajongs in the State of Arunachal Pradesh. The NHRC approached this Court by way of a Writ Petition (C) No.720 of 1995 titled "National Human Rights Commission vs. State of Arunachal Pradesh" seeking direction from this Court to ensure that the Chakmas and Hajongs are not forcibly ousted from the State of Arunachal Pradesh, which was disposed of on 9th January, 1996[1]. In the said case, the Union of India appeared before this Court and stated that decision to settle the Chakmas in the State of Arunachal Pradesh was taken after discussion between the Government of India and the North-East Frontier Agency ("NEFA") Administration (Predecessor of the State of Arunachal Pradesh). The Chakmas were residing in the State of Arunachal Pradesh for more than three decades and had close social, religious and economic ties. As per joint statement issued by the Prime Ministers of India and Bangladesh in February, 1972, the Union Government took a decision to confer citizenship on the Chakmas under Section 5(1)(a) of the Citizenship Act, 1955 but the State of Arunachal Pradesh had reservations on this count. The Central Government was in favour of a dialogue between the State Government, the Chakmas and all concerned to resolve the issue of granting citizenship while also redressing the genuine grievances of citizens of Arunachal Pradesh. The stand of the State of Arunachal

Pradesh was that it had provided basic amenities to the Chakmas but the State had a right to ask the Chakmas to quit the State. The State could not permit outsiders to settle within its territory as it had limited resources and the Union of India had refused to share its responsibility. The Deputy Commissioner of the area was to forward the applications for citizenship after due inquiry but no such application was pending. Further stand of the State was that settlement of Chakmas will disturb its ethnic balance and destroy its culture and identity. The tribals of the State consider Chakmas as potential threat to their tradition and culture.

3. This Court considered rival submissions and held that the Chakmas apprehend threat on the All Arunachal Pradesh Students' Union ("AAPSU") who were reported to be enforcing economic blockades on the refugee camps, adversely affecting supply of ration, medical and essential facilities to the Chakmas. Some Chakmas had died on account of blockade. This Court further noticed that Chakmas could invoke Section 5(1)(a) of the Citizenship Act by filing application in form prescribed by Part II of the Citizenship Rules, 1956. The observations in NHRC case (supra), inter alia, are as follows :-

> "18. From what we have said hereinbefore, there is no doubt that the Chakmas who migrated from East Pakistan (now Bangladesh) in 1964, first settled down in the State of Assam and then shifted to areas which now fall within the State of Arunachal Pradesh. They have settled there since the last about two and a half decades and have raised their families in the said State. Their

children have married and they too have had children. Thus, a large number of them were born in the State itself. Now it is proposed to uproot them by force. The AAPSU has been giving out threats to forcibly drive them out to the neighbouring State which in turn is unwilling to accept them. The residents of the neighbouring State have also threatened to kill them if they try to enter their State. They are thus sandwiched between two forces, each pushing in opposite direction which can only hurt them. Faced with the prospect of annihilation the NHRC was moved, which, finding it impossible to extend protection to them, moved this Court for certain reliefs.

19. By virtue of their long and prolonged stay in the State, the Chakmas who migrated to, and those born in the State, seek citizenship under the Constitution read with Section 5 of the Act. We have already indicated earlier that if a person satisfies the requirements of Section 5 of the Act, he/she can be registered as a citizen of India. The procedure to be followed in processing such requests has been outlined in Part II of the Rules. We have adverted to the relevant rules hereinbefore. According to these Rules, the application for registration has to be made in the prescribed form, duly affirmed, to the Collector within whose jurisdiction he resides. After the application is so received, the authority to register a person as a citizen of India, is vested in the officer named under Rule 8 of the Rules. Under Rule 9, the Collector is expected to transmit every application under Section 5(1)(a) of the Act to the Central Government.

On a conjoint reading of Rules 8 and 9 it becomes clear that the Collector has merely to receive the application and forward it to the Central Government. It is only the authority constituted under Rule 8 which is empowered to register a person as a citizen of India. It follows that only that authority can refuse to entertain an application made under Section 5 of the Act. Yet it is an admitted fact that after receipt of the application, the Deputy Collector (DC) makes an enquiry and if the report is adverse, the DC refuses to forward the application; in other words, he rejects the application at the threshold and does not forward it to the Central Government. The grievance of the Central Government is that since the DC does not forward the applications, it is not in a position to take a decision whether or not to register the person as a citizen of India. That is why it is said that the DC or Collector, who receives the application should be directed to forward the same to the Central Government to enable it to decide the request on merits. It is obvious that by refusing to forward the applications of the Chakmas to the Central Government, the DC is failing in his duty and is also preventing the Central Government from performing its duty under the Act and the Rules.

20. We are a country governed by the Rule of Law. Our Constitution confers certain rights on every human being and certain other rights on citizens. Every person is entitled to equality before the law and equal protection of the laws. So also, no person can be deprived of

his life or personal liberty except according to procedure established by law. Thus the State is bound to protect the life and liberty of every human being, be he a citizen or otherwise, and it cannot permit any body or group of persons, e.g., the AAPSU, to threaten the Chakmas to leave the State, failing which they would be forced to do so. No State Government worth the name can tolerate such threats by one group of persons to another group of persons; it is duty- bound to protect the threatened group from such assaults and if it fails to do so, it will fail to perform its constitutional as well as statutory obligations. Those giving such threats would be liable to be dealt with in accordance with law. The State Government must act impartially and carry out its legal obligations to safeguard the life, health and well-being of Chakmas residing in the State without being inhibited by local politics. Besides, by refusing to forward their applications, the Chakmas are denied rights, constitutional and statutory, to be considered for being registered as citizens of India."

4. Accordingly, direction was issued to the State of Arunachal Pradesh to ensure that life and liberty of Chakmas residing in the State was protected against any attempt to evict them by organized groups such as AAPSU and their applications could be forwarded to the Central Government.
5. Case of the petitioners, further is that the application of the State of Arunachal Pradesh for modification and Writ Petition (C) No.593 of 1997 filed by an organization of tribals of Arunachal Pradesh against the judgment of this Court was

also dismissed. Another writ petition being Writ Petition No.13 of 1998 against the judgment of this Court was dismissed on 9th December, 2002. Thereafter applications were filed for citizenship but the same were not acted upon. The Election Commission of India in the light of judgment of this Court passed orders dated 3rd March, 2004 declaring the resolution dated 14th May, 2003 passed by the State of Arunachal Pradesh against facilities to the petitioners to be unconstitutional but the authorities of the State of Arunachal Pradesh had not forwarded the applications as required under Rule 9 of the Citizenship Rules to the Central Government.

6. Counter affidavit has been filed by the Union of India stating that the applications directly received by the Ministry of Home Affairs were forwarded to the Government of Arunachal Pradesh which had not been returned except few applications with negative recommendations. The said applications were returned back to the Government of Arunachal Pradesh. Ministry of Home Affairs had advised the Government of Arunachal Pradesh to act in compliance with the judgment of this Court.

7. The stand of the State of Arunachal Pradesh is that there was no threat to the life and liberty of the Chakmas and Hajong refugees. After receiving the judgment of this Court, the judgment was circulated to Inspector General of Police, Deputy Commissioners of the concerned Districts and Principal Chief Conservator of Forests. The State Government was fully bound by the direction of this Court and had taken all necessary steps to comply with the same. The State of Arunachal Pradesh had received 4382

applications. Though the popular sentiment of the indigenous tribals was different, the State of Arunachal Pradesh was honouring the order of this Court. It is further stated that Chakmas and Hajong tribes were settled in NEFA from 1964 to 1969 when there were no elected bodies in the State of Arunachal Pradesh. The laws applicable in the State of Arunachal Pradesh like the Government of India Act, 1870, the Bengal Eastern Frontier Regulation, 1873, the Scheduled District Act, 1874, the Assam Frontier Tract Regulation, 1880, the Assam Frontier Forest Regulation, 1891, the Chin Hills Regulations, 1896 and the Assam Frontier (Administration of Justice) Regulation, 1945 (1 of 1945) were not taken into account. One thousand four hundred ninety seven Chakmas have been included in the electoral rolls.

8. The petitioners have filed a rejoinder affidavit alleging that children of Chakmas and Hajongs are denied educational facilities. They were not being covered by the public distribution system. They presented a petition to the 10th LokSabha and also to RajyaSabha Committee on Petitions. The said Committee in its 105th Report published on 14th August, 1997 made recommendation to grant Indian Citizenship to the Chakmas but the said recommendation has not been acted upon. The recommendation is as follows :

> "42. The Committee, therefore, recommends that the Chakmas of Arunachal Pradesh who came there prior to 25.3.1971 be granted Indian citizenship. The Committee also recommends that those Chakmas who have been born in India should also be considered for Indian citizenship. The Committee further

recommends that the fate of those Chakmas who came to the State after 25.3.1971 be discussed and decided by the Central Government and State Government Jointly. The Committees also recommends that all the old applications of Chakmas for citizenship which have either been rejected or withheld by Deputy Commissioners or the State Deputy Commissioner or the State Government continue to block the forwarding of such applications to Central Government, the Central Government may consider to incorporate necessary provision in the Rules (or the Act it so required) whereby it could directly receive, consider and decide the application for citizenship in the 23 case of Chakmas of Arunachal Pradesh. The Committee also recommends that Chakmas be also considered for granting them the status of Scheduled Tribes at the time of granting the citizenship. The Committee would like to earnestly urge upon the Central Government and State Government to ensure that until amicable solution is arrived at, the Chakmas are allowed to stay in Arunachal Pradesh with full protection and safety, honour and dignity".

9. When the matter came up for hearing before this Court on 1st August, 2012, the following order was passed:-

"Mr. B. Bhattacharyya, learned Additional Solicitor General for respondent No. 5, and Mr. Anil Shrivastav, learned counsel for respondent Nos. 1 to 4, pray for some time to seek instructions and also to ensure that the controversy raised in the Writ Petition is resolved at the hands of the Central Government and the State Government at the earliest."

10. Again on 28th August, 2012, following order was passed : "Mr. B. Bhattacharyya, learned Additional Solicitor General appearing for the respondent No. 5 - Union of India, submits that all 4637 applications for grant of citizenship in respect of Chakmas received in the Ministry of Home Affairs, Government of India have been returned to the State Government as the applications were not made to the appropriate authority in prescribed form and were also not accompanied with the recommendations of the State Government as per statutory requirement.

    Having regard to the decision of this Court in National Human Rights Commission Vs. State of Arunachal Pradesh and Another, (1996) 1 SCC 742, and the directions contained therein, we direct the State of Arunachal Pradesh to submit a comprehensive report/affidavit to this Court in respect of 4637 applications returned by the Central Government to the State Government on the following aspects in respect of each application:-

    (i) Whether the conditions laid down in the relevant clauses of Section 5 of the Citizenship Act, 1955 (for short, 'Act') are satisfied;

    (ii) Whether the applicant has an intention to make India his permanent home;

    (iii) Whether the applicant has signed oath of allegiance as specified in the Second Schedule to the Act; and

    (iv) Whether the applicant is of good character and is otherwise a fit and proper person to be registered as a citizen of India.

    The above report/affidavit shall be submitted by

the State of Arunachal Pradesh to this Court through the Secretary (Political), Government of Arunachal Pradesh within two months from today.

A copy of the report/affidavit shall be given to the Advocate-on- Record for the petitioners well in advance."

11. On 20th January, 2014, this Court passed the following Order:

    "List the matter on 5th May, 2014, so as to enable the Joint High Powered Committee constituted vide Government of India's Order No.13/2/2010-NE-II dated 10/08/2010. to place on record the progress made in the matter.

    We are sure that the Committee would make all efforts so that the work entrusted to it is concluded preferably before the next date of hearing."

12. Additional Affidavit dated 2nd January, 2013 was filed by the State of Arunachal Pradesh stating that the Government of India, Ministry of Home Affairs (N.E. Division) has constituted a committee under the Chairmanship of Joint Secretary (N.E.), Ministry of Home Affairs on 10th August, 2010 to examine various issues relating to settlement of Chakmas/Hajongs in Arunachal Pradesh including the possibility of granting Indian citizenship to eligible Chakmas/ Hajongs. The Committee has held its sitting on 9th January, 2012 and taken certain decisions. Thus, the issue was not being ignored though there was no delay in the matter.

13. We have heard learned counsel for the parties and perused the record.

14. Learned counsel for the petitioners submitted that their rights have been duly acknowledged by this

Court in NHRC case (supra). Still, their legitimate right of citizenship has not so far materialized. They have been settled after a conscious decision at the highest level of the Government of India. They could not be treated as foreigners. He has placed reliance on a judgment of the Gauhati High Court dated 19th March, 2013 in PIL No.52 of 2010 titled "All Arunachal Pradesh Students Union (AAPSU) vs. The Election Commission of India" dismissing a petition filed by AAPSU against the guidelines issued by the Election Commission of India for revision of electoral rolls in respect of areas where there is substantial presence of Chakmas and Hajongs. In the said judgment, the Memorandum dated 23rd March, 2005 issued by the Election Commission of India and further guidelines dated 3rd October, 2007 for revision of electoral rolls with reference to 1st January, 2007 as qualifying date are also referred to. The objection against the Chakmas being treated as ordinary residents of Arunachal Pradesh in absence of possession of valid Inner Line Passes was also considered. The Election Commission of India supported its guidelines with guidelines with reference to a judgment of the Delhi High Court dated 28th September, 2000 in W.P. No.886 of 2000 (Peoples Union for Civil Liberties vs. Election Commission of India &Ors.)

15. In the judgment of the Gauhati High Court, it was noted that in contradiction to those unwanted illegal migrants who sneak into the country, the Chakmas migrated to India on account of their displacement and the Government of India agreed to grant them citizenship. In these circumstances, the guidelines of the Government of India were held to be justified and did not warrant any

requirement of Inner Line permit. The relevant observations are:

> "[18] .... Having regard to the facts and circumstances which have been also highlighted by the Hon'ble Supreme Court as referred to above in NRHC case, we are of the view that these additional guidelines, having been issued in the peculiar circumstances obtaining, cannot be held to be discriminatory.

Further, in view of the policy decision taken by the Government of India to settle the Chakma refugees in different States and also in Arunachal Pradesh in consultation with the authorities of the Arunachal Pradesh, and also to confer Indian citizenship, the contention of the petitioners that the aforesaid guidelines have the effect of violating the provisions of law in terms of lack of Inner Line Permit or violation of provisions of section 13 of the Registration of Births and Deaths Act, 1969 does not hold water. We are of the view that once a decision had been taken to settle these Chakma refugees in Arunachal Pradesh in consultation with the authorities of Arunachal Pradcsh, they would become residents of Arunachal Pradesh and would not require the Inner Line Permit/Pass. Otherwise also, once they have been allowed to settle in Arunachal Pradesh, it would be deemed that such permits had been granted to them and in our considered opinion, any other view would negate and defeat the policy decision taken by the Government of India in consultation with the Arunachal Pradesh authorities to settle these Chakmas in Arunachal Pradesh.

Similarly, as regards, the other contention of the petitioners that the guidelines would contravene the provisions of section 13 of the Registration of Births and Deaths Act, 1969 also cannot be accepted. It may be noted that the Chakmas had taken refuge in this country under distress and trying circumstances after having been uprooted from their hearth and homes and made to flee to avoid persecution. Further, later on, after having allowed to settle in Arunachal Pradesh, they had faced difficulties and harassments from the neighbouring local populace which had been taken note of by the Supreme Court in NHRC case as mentioned above. Therefore, issuing of the additional guidelines for the purpose of verification of the birth of the claimants on the basis of other credible materials for the purpose of enrolment in the electoral rolls where these Chakmas had been officially settled cannot be interfered with merely on the technical ground that certain provisions of Registration of Births and Deaths Act, 1969 have not been strictly complied with, if the evidences are otherwise credible and trustworthy.

We are of the view that the additional guidelines which had been issued by the Election Commission of India are merely to enable those Chakmas to enjoy such benefits as a citizen of this Country including the right to vote by having their names enrolled in the electoral rolls of the concerned constituency where they have been settled. Once, these Chakma refugees have been granted citizenship, they are entitled to enjoy all the rights and privileges that flow on becoming a citizen of this country and further, they are entitled to have their rights as citizens of this country protected and safeguarded."

16. We find merit in the contention of the petitioners. It stands acknowledged by this Court on the basis

of stand of the Government of India that the Chakmas have a right to be granted citizenship subject to the procedure being followed. It also stands recognized by judicial decisions that they cannot be required to obtain any Inner Line permit as they are settled in the State of Arunachal Pradesh.

17. In State of Arunachal Pradesh vs. KhudiramChakma[2], this Court noted the ancient history of Arunachal Pradesh as follows:

> "41. The history of the mountainous and multitribal north-east frontier region which is now known as Arunachal Pradesh ascends for hundreds of years into the mists of tradition and mythology. According to Pauranic legend, Rukmini, the daughter of King Bhishmak, was carried away on the eve of her marriage by Lord Krishna himself. The ruins of the fort at Bhalukpung are claimed by the Akas as the original home of their ancestor Bhaluka, the grandson of Bana Raja, who was defeated by Lord Krishna at Tezpur (Assam). A Kalita King, Ramachandra, driven from his kingdom in the plains of Assam, fled to the Dafla (now Nishang) foothills and established there his capital of Mayapore, which is identified with the ruins on the Ita hill. A place of great sanctity in the beautiful lower reaches of the Lohit River, the Brahmakund, where Parasuram opened a passage through the hills with a single blow of his mighty axe, still attracts the Hindu pilgrims from all over the country."

18. The above history shows the integral link of the State of Arunachal Pradesh with the rest of the country since ancient times. It is well known that

the Chakmas and Hajongs were displaced from the area which became part of East Pakistan (now in Bangladesh) on construction of Kaptai Dam and were allowed to be rehabilitated under the decision of the Government of India. As earlier held by this Court, the Delhi High Court and Gauhati High Court, they need to be protected and their claims of citizenship need to be considered as per applicable procedure. They could not be discriminated against in any manner pending formal conferment of rights of citizenship. Their status also stands duly acknowledged in the guidelines of the Election Commission of India.

19. Learned Additional Solicitor General fairly stated that the Government of India will earnestly take appropriate measures in the matter, granted some more time.

20. Accordingly, we allow this petition and direct the Government of India and the State of Arunachal Pradesh to finalise the conferment of citizenship rights on eligible Chakmas and Hajongs and also to ensure compliance of directions in judicial decisions referred to in earlier part of this order for protection of their life and liberty and against their discrimination in any manner. The exercise may be completed at the earliest preferably within three months from today.

..................................J.

[ANIL R. DAVE] J.

[ADARSH KUMAR GOEL]

NEW DELHI SEPTEMBER 17, 2015

[1] (1996) 1 SCC 742 [2] (1994) Supp. 1 SCC 615

APPENDIX IV

JOINT-ACTION-COMMITTEE

CRDO-CCRCHAP-APCGBA-APCSU-APHSU-CWWS-CNCIAP-RCTS
Head Office: Diyun, Dist. Changlang, Arunachal Pradesh – 792103
Email:-jointactioncommittee.ch@gmail.com Contact No. +91-9880219545, +91-7005574659

JAC Member Organisations

1. Chakma Rights and Development Organisation
2. Committee for Citizenship Rights of the Chakmas & Hajongs of Arunachal Pradesh
3. Arunachal Pradesh Chakma Gaonburah Association
4. Arunachal Pradesh Chakma Students' Union
5. Arunachal Pradesh Hajong Students' Union
6. Chakma Women Welfare Society
7. Chakma National Council of India – Arunachal Pradesh
8. Rashtriya Chakma Tribal Sangha

No. JAC/MHA/02-2022 20.02.2022

Shri Amit Shah Ji,
Hon'ble Minister of Home Affairs, Govt of India
Central Secretariat, North Block, New Delhi -110001

Sub:- Permanent Resolution of long pending Chakma-Hajong issue of Arunachal Pradesh

Ref:- Your Meeting with Chakma-Hajong delegation on 20thFebruary 2020 at Itanagar, Arunachal Pradesh for permanent resolution of Chakma-Hajong issue

Dear Sir,

As we celebrate the golden jubilee marking the 50th year of the naming of Arunachal Pradesh from the North-East Frontier Agency (NEFA) and the political status as an Union Territory, beginning its journey into self-governance, the Joint Action Committee of all the Chakma & Hajong NGOs are writing to you with a particular emphasis for **permanent resolution of long pending Chakma-Hajong issue of Arunachal Pradesh.**

After independence, this land has witnessed unfolding of series of administrative, political & strategic policy decisions. From governing of NEFA based on the Elwin Verrier's "A Philosophy for NEFA" to administrating it as an "Excluded Area" with minimum interference through the Governor of Assam to governing it through the Ministry of External Affairs and then Ministry of Home Affairs and then granting of the political status as Union Territory, Arunachal Pradesh has come a long way.

JOINT-ACTION-COMMITTEE

CRDO-CCRCHAP-APCGBA-APCSU-APHSU-CWWS-CNCIAP-RCTS
Head Office: Diyun, Dist. Changlang, Arunachal Pradesh – 792103
Email:-jointactioncommittee.ch@gmail.com Contact No. +91-9880219545, +91-7005574659

It is high time that the historical residual issues of the state resolved once and for all in conformity with the vision of Hon'ble Prime Minister to make NE region free from all the pending issues. Chakma-Hajong long pending issue is one such historical residual issue that deserves your kind attention for permanent solution in the greater interest of the state/nation.

In this regard, a Chakma-Hajong delegation had a meeting with you on 20th February 2020 during the Arunachal Pradesh Statehood Day at Itanagar wherein you had assured us of permanent resolution of Chakma and Hajong issue once and for all before Diwali 2020.

(1) Historical perspective of Chakma-Hajong issue:-

It is an established fact that the scheme for rehabilitation of Chakmas & Hajongs in NEFA, now Arunachal Pradesh was initiated by the NEFA Administration following high level policy decision after the Chinese aggression in 1962 as part of strategic policy decision. According to the Ministry of Home Affairs in the Public Account Committee (1977-78) the objectives of the scheme of Resettlement in NEFA were as follows:-

(a) The North-East Frontier Agency (now Arunachal Pradesh) is comparatively thinly populated; the then overall density of population being about 11 persons per sq. mile.

(b) A population vacuum near the border may result in attempts by hostile neighbour to take advantage of the situation.

(c) A settled community along the border will be a positive deterrent against the temptation of infiltration from across the border.

(d) The actual presence of a settled community along the border would further reduce the scope of any border dispute.

(e) A progressive community will boost up the morale of the local inhabitants and inspire greater zeal for accelerated economic progress.

(f) The settlement of people belonging to mixed community in NEFA may help towards emotional integration of NEFA people with the rest of the country.

JOINT-ACTION-COMMITTEE

CRDO-CCRCHAP-APCGBA-APCSU-APHSU-CWWS-CNCIAP-RCTS
Head Office: Diyun, Dist. Changlang, Arunachal Pradesh – 792103
Email:-jointactioncommittee.ch@gmail.com Contact No. +91-9880219545, +91-7005574659

(2) Post-Rehabilitation pangs and politicization of Chakma-Hajong issue in Arunachal Pradesh:

In keeping with the strategic and administrative objectives, the Chakmas and Hajongs who were displaced from erstwhile East Pakistan took refuge in India and were taken to the remote jungles of NEFA, now Arunachal Pradesh for resettlement and rehabilitation. The last transit camp was at Ledo, Assam after which they were settled permanently by the Government of India in the erstwhile NEFA (now Arunachal Pradesh) with the consent of the local administration and tribal leaders /chiefs.

The Chakmas-Hajongs of AP continued to exercise all rights and privileges as citizens of India till the 1980s when the newly formed state of Arunachal Pradesh, under the influence of the foreigners agitation of Assam erroneously mis-identified the Chakmas-Hajongs as foreigners and for reasons best known to political dispensation of the time, systematically began to take away the rights of Chakmas and Hajongs one after another and left no stone unturned to evict the Chakmas-Hajongs from Arunachal Pradesh through overt and covert means by state and non-state actors.

Another reason for the victimization of the Chakmas and Hajongs is best described in terms of the findings of Dr. Nicholas Christakis, the noted sociologist and physician who was named among the top 100 most influential people by Time magazine in 2009. He explains that "In order to band together, we need a common enemy". Now, the fact is, whereas most Indian states have been linguistically organised, Arunachal Pradesh comprising 26 major tribes and more than 100 subtribes is a rare exception and thus lacked a pan-Arunachali identity. The (mis)-identification of the Chakmas and Hajongs as the "other", provided the required "enemy", so crucial to create a pan-Arunachali identity. However, the innocent Chakmas and Hajongs caught at the receiving end of this bargain found their rights derecognized day by day as various student groups and political parties picked up this misinformed propaganda to further their political careers.

JOINT-ACTION-COMMITTEE

CRDO-CCRCHAP-APCGBA-APCSU-APHSU-CWWS-CNCIAP-RCTS
Head Office: Diyun, Dist. Changlang, Arunachal Pradesh – 792103
Email:-jointactioncommittee.ch@gmail.com Contact No. +91-9880219545, +91-7005574659

(3) Relocation is not an acceptable solution, it would multiply the problems many-fold and take Chakma-Hajong community 57 years back in time.

(i) It has been 57 long years since the Chakmas and Hajongs had already been rehabilitated in Arunachal Pradesh with 5 acres of land allotted to each family to start life afresh as citizens this country. For most of second generation and current generation born in India, this is the only place which they can call their own. This is their birthplace and motherland.

(ii) About 90-95% of Chakmas and Hajongs are citizens of India by birth under section 3 (1) (a) of the Citizenship Act of 1955 and as such are entitled to fundamental rights as guaranteed under Part III of the constitution. Even those original migrants, who constitute no more than 5-10% of the population today, are legally protected as there is a ruling from the Hon'ble Supreme Court of India in 1996 and 2015 to grant citizenship rights, which is yet to be implemented.

(iii) Unlike the Tibetan refugees who prefer to remain in India as 'honoured guests', the Chakmas and Hajong refugees have been brought and rehabilitated by the Government of India with the intention of permanent settlement and were duly resettled in NEFA, then administered by the Centre directly through the governor of Assam. Hence, the arrival of the Chakmas/Hajongs predates the formation of Arunachal Pradesh. Uprooting them is not only morally and ethically wrong but a breach of that promise.

(iv) The Chakmas and Hajongs have been legally settled there by the Government of India in consultation with erstwhile NEFA administration (now Arunachal Pradesh) during 1964-69 and lands were allotted in consultation with local tribes which is clearly in consonance with section 7 of Bengal Eastern Frontier Regulation, 1873. The Hon'ble Guwahati High Court in AAPSU v/s Election Commission of India, in 2013 held that Bengal Eastern Frontier Regulation Act, 1873 is not applicable to Chakma-Hajongs stating that

JOINT-ACTION-COMMITTEE

CRDO-CCRCHAP-APCGBA-APCSU-APHSU-CWWS-CNCIAP-RCTS
Head Office: Diyun, Dist. Changlang, Arunachal Pradesh – 792103
Email:-jointactioncommittee.ch@gmail.com Contact No. +91-9880219545, +91-7005574659

"once they are allowed to settle in A.P, it would be deemed that such permits (Inner Line Permit) had been granted to them and in our considered opinion, any other view would negate and defeat the policy decision taken by the Government in consultation with the Arunachal Pradesh Govt authorities to settle the Chakmas in AP"

(v) The North-East in general and Arunachal Pradesh in particular is inhabited by multitude of tribal groups belonging to different language, ethnic composition. Relocating the Chakmas and Hajongs to other state 57 years after their rehabilitation in Arunachal Pradesh may open up ethnic fault lines and create more problems that can destabilize the region.

(vi) It is true that Citizenship Amendment Act (CAA) of 2019 is exempted in ILP states and 6th Schedule areas and so it is not technically applicable to the Chakmas and Hajongs of AP. However, the intent of CAA was to grant citizenship to non-Muslim persecuted Buddhist, Hindu, Jain, Christian, Sikh and Parsi minorities from Pakistan, Bangladesh and Afghanistan who came to India as recent as 31.12.2014. If the recent illegal migrants can be granted citizenship under CAA, how can one imagine that the Chakma and Hajongs of 1964 who were rehabilitated legally more than half a century ago be given a raw deal and uprooted /relocated now in a democratic republic like India?

(vii) The Chakmas and Hajongs have built their hearth and homes, reared domestic animals and livestock, nurtured various crops, and developed plantations. During the last 6 decades, they assimilated /integrated/ shared many cultural practices - religious, spiritual, and material exchanges and even engaged in matrimonial relationships with local populace.

(viii) Buddhist Chakmas and Hindu Hajongs have been one of the most loyal tribes of India, who are socially, linguistically, and culturally closer to Indian civilization ethos and can act as a sentinel in the border areas.

JOINT-ACTION-COMMITTEE

CRDO-CCRCHAP-APCGBA-APCSU-APHSU-CWWS-CNCIAP-RCTS
Head Office: Diyun, Dist. Changlang, Arunachal Pradesh – 792103
Email:-jointactioncommittee.ch@gmail.com Contact No. +91-9880219545, +91-7005574659

(4) False propaganda and xenophobia against Chakma-Hajongs:-

We now seek your august intervention to consider the need to clear the air on so-called Chakma Hajong 'abnormal population growth'/ 'illegal influx' and also address concerns around dilution of tribal rights / protection of indigenous rights. This is a pre-requisite towards a permanent resolution of the vexed issue.

One of the allegations levelled against Chakmas-Hajongs has been the complaint that there is an 'abnormal' rise of Chakma population and that the 'demographic' profile of the state will be adversely affected. Nothing can be far from truth. In fact, as per study done based on the Census data available in public domain, the annual growth rate of Chakma population is lower (2.6%) than the overall annual growth rate of population of the state which stood at 2.87% (50-year period). The decadal growth rate for Chakma-Hajong population was 17% for the decade 2001-2011 as against the overall decadal growth rate of 26% for the state. So, abnormal population growth is only a myth that create animosity and is the root cause of all anti-Chakma sentiments. It must be settled through a data-driven approach by the centre.

Once the issue of population has been cleared, we can move to the next step towards finding a permanent solution.

(5) Solution Proposals:

(i) **Assimilation / Integration based:** It is an evolutionary historical approach to find a solution of the issue through assimilation/integration. A fact-based approach, built on Indian constitutional ethos of unity and diversity, it is built on mutual respect and tolerance for each other. In fact, the foreigner issue in the parent state of Assam was resolved using the dimension of 'time' - 25 March 1971 being used as the cut-off date. A similar guiding principle can be formulated in Arunachal Pradesh too. However, it is predicated upon the acceptance of and restoration of all rights including ST and PRC rights to Chakmas and Hajongs as it recognizes

JOINT-ACTION-COMMITTEE

CRDO-CCRCHAP-APCGBA-APCSU-APHSU-CWWS-CNCIAP-RCTS
Head Office: Diyun, Dist. Changlang, Arunachal Pradesh – 792103
Email:-jointactioncommittee.ch@gmail.com Contact No. +91-9880219545, +91-7005574659

equal rights for all tribes and empower them to flourish in a spirit of mutual respect and solidarity, not of conflict. It is the ideal solution to resolve the issue because once the Chakma Hajongs are accepted as integral part of the state and due rights are restored to them, there will be a sea change in the minds and heart of all communities as they would all be treated 'equal' in the eyes of all and therefore promote tribal solidarity and fraternity amongst various communities based on multi-culturalism. In fact, the Chakmas and Hajong themselves are bound to feel more Indian and become more responsible as citizens.

Restoration of rights also implies:

(a) Revocation of circular No. Pol-21/81 dtd. 29 Sep 1980 and restore access to employment rights in state government to all Chakma-Hajong citizens of India by birth.

(b) Revoke FP-5D/90-91 dated 31 Oct 1991 and pass necessary instruction to the Ministry of Food and Civil Supplies to re-start issue of Ration cards and PDS items to all Chakmas /Hajongs.

(c) Withdraw the impugned circular No.16045-67 dated 11 Oct 1994 and restore the pride of the Chakma/Hajong Gaon Burah(headman) by issuing a fresh order of appointment of Chakma/ Hajong Gaon Burahs as village Panchayat authorities at par with and in line with the Arunachal Pradesh Panchayati Raj Act, 1997.

(d) Direct the state government to withdraw the circular No. DYN-JUD1/97 dated 31 Oct 1997 and allow free flow of goods and labour services involving all communities including the Chakma/ Hajong people in village work, contract and business without any discrimination

(e) Take necessary actions to recognize and issue PRC/ST certificates to Chakmas & Hajongs who are citizens of India by birth based on the 105th Rajya Sabha Petition Committee recommendations and the fact that Chakmas/Hajongs domiciled in all Indian states are recognized as Scheduled

JOINT-ACTION-COMMITTEE

CRDO-CCRCHAP-APCGBA-APCSU-APHSU-CWWS-CNCIAP-RCTS

Head Office: Diyun, Dist. Changlang, Arunachal Pradesh – 792103

Email:-jointactioncommittee.ch@gmail.com Contact No. +91-9880219545, +91-7005574659

Tribes. A separate quota for ST (Plains) and ST (Hills) may be created based on specified criteria to address concerns around dilution of rights for local indigenous tribes.

(f) Necessary instructions be passed to extend the flagship MGNREGA to all the 45 Chakma and Hajong villages so that they can take part in the nation building process by being active participants in the scheme. Also, the Chakmas & Hajongs should be given access to all other Central /State Government schemes, as applicable from time to time.

(g) Enrolment of all Eligible Chakma Voters: Elector population ratio for Chakma villages is the lowest at 7.7% as against the state average of 55% and despite repeated requests for inclusion, the situation has not improved. EROs must include all such eligible Chakma and Hajong voters without any prejudice.

(h) Raise a Chakma/Hajong Battalion to channelize the energies of loyal Indian Chakma/Hajong youths to serve the Indian Army with great pride and fervour.

(ii) Separation/ Autonomy based: In case option 5 (i) is not feasible, the other option available is to carve out a separate territorial area in the form of an Autonomous Council for the Chakmas/ Hajongs in AP and have it directly administered /governed by the Central Government in the existing settlement areas under the 6th schedule of the Centre.

(6) Prayer:-

The Chakma and Hajong tribal people have been the worst victims of partition and have always been pro-Indian andloyal to India. They have suffered long enough for many decades and at least 3 generations have been affected and deprived of their due rights and entitlements. They have knocked every door and exhausted almost all options and cannot afford to suffer another round of mass migration and relocation 57 years after their rehabilitation. We call upon the Centre under your able leadership to create conditions and issue

JOINT-ACTION-COMMITTEE

CRDO-CCRCHAP-APCGBA-APCSU-APHSU-CWWS-CNCIAP-RCTS
Head Office: Diyun, Dist. Changlang, Arunachal Pradesh – 792103
Email:-jointactioncommittee.ch@gmail.com Contact No. +91-9880219545, +91-7005574659

necessary directions to the state for the restoration of rights and development of the Chakmas and Hajongs like any other communities of the state and provide them the space to integrate fully and allow them to live with dignity and honour in Arunachal Pradesh and contribute to the overall progress of the state as responsible citizens of this great nation.

JAI HIND!

Sincerely,

Mahendra Chakma
Co-Chairman, JAC &
President, CRDO
Mobile No. +91-9880219545
Email:-
mahendra.chakma@gmail.com

Subimal Bikash Chakma
Co-Chairman, JAC &
President, CCRCHAP
Mobile No. +91-7005574659
Email:-
sbnizoom@gmail.com

APPENDIX V

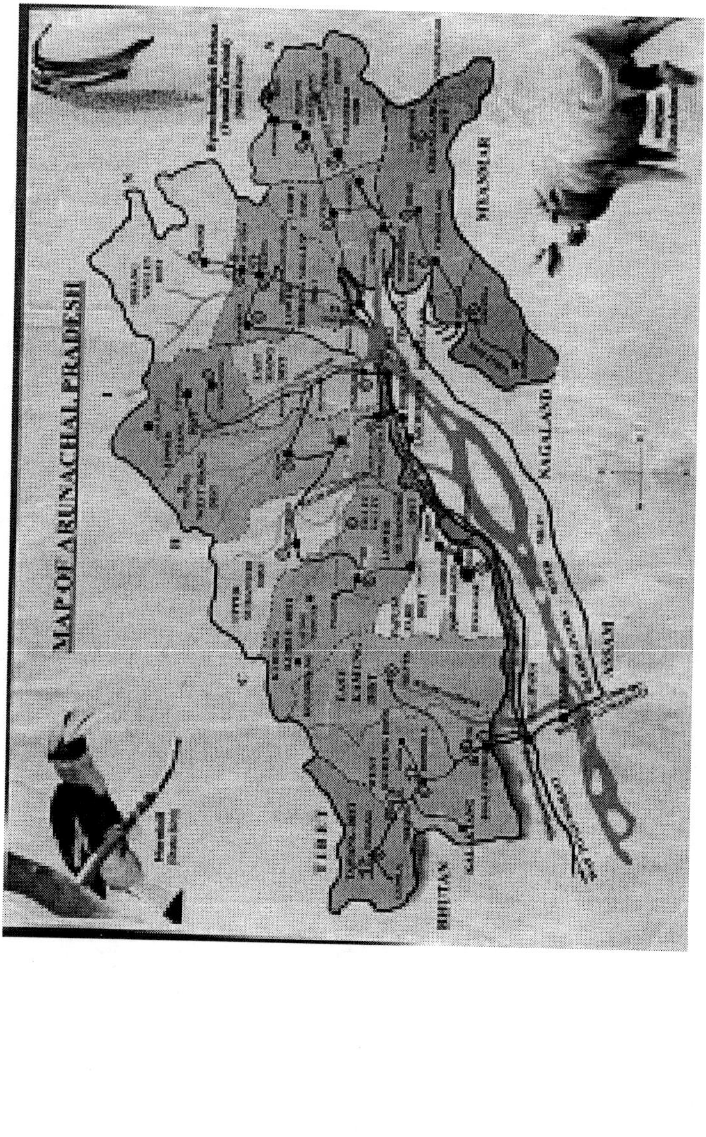
MAP OF ARUNACHAL PRADESH
TIBET
BHUTAN
ASSAM
NAGALAND
MYANMAR

APPENDIX VI

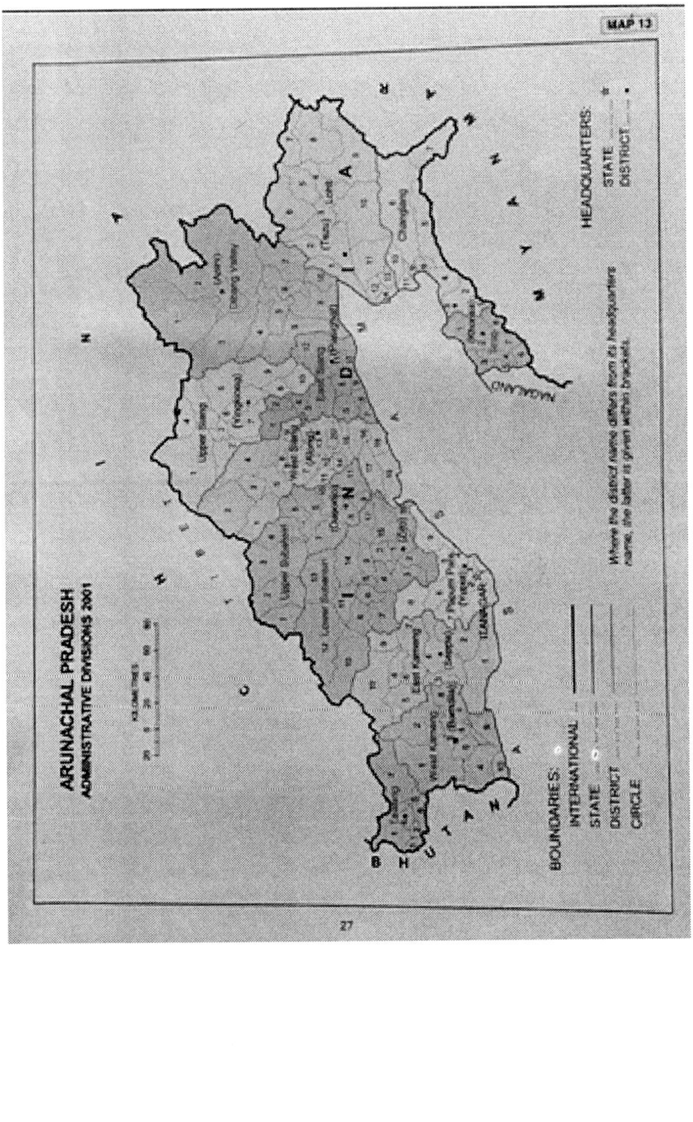
MAP 13
ARUNACHAL PRADESH
ADMINISTRATIVE DIVISIONS 2001
BOUNDARIES:
INTERNATIONAL
STATE
DISTRICT
CIRCLE
HEADQUARTERS:
STATE
DISTRICT
NAGALAND
27

APPENDIX VII

गृह मंत्री
भारत
नई दिल्ली-११०००१
HOME MINISTER
INDIA
NEW DELHI-110001

No. V-[illegible]/92-HMP

Dear Shri Chitta Basu,

I am in receipt of your letter dated the 7th October, 1992 enclosing a report from the Peoples' Rights Organisation on the question of Indian citizenship rights of the stateless Chakmas and Hajongs of Arunachal Pradesh.

I am having the matter looked into.

With regards.

Yours sincerely,

(S.B. CHAVAN)

Shri Chitta Basu, MP.
28, Gurdwara Rakabganj Road.
NEW DELHI.

APPENDIX VIII

CHITTA BASU
MEMBER OF PARLIAMENT
LOK SABHA

Phone : [illegible]
25, Gurdwara Rakabganj Road
New Delhi-110001

Dated : 14.3.1993.

Dear Prime Minister,

I enclose herewith a Memorandum from Shri Subimal Bikash Chakma, President, Committee for Citizenship Rights of the Chakmas of Arunachal Pradesh regarding the grant of Indian citizenship for Chakmas and Hajongs of Arunachal Pradesh.

I shall be very much glad if you kindly get the matter properly examined and take necessary action for the protection of rights of Chakmas and Hajongs of Arunachal Pradesh.

With best regards,

Yours sincerely,

Encls: As above.

(CHITTA BASU)

Shri P.V. Narasimha Rao,
Prime Minister,
Govt. of India,
NEW DELHI.

Copy to:- Shri Subimal Bikash Chakma, President, Committee for ~~to~~ Citizenship Rights of the Chakmas of Arunachal Pradesh, Ashok Buddha Vihar, Old Power House Road, Rajghat, New Delhi-110002.

APPENDIX IX

New Delhi
April 8, 1992

Dear Shri Chatterjee,

I have received your letter of March 31, 1992 enclosing a representation from the Committee for Citizenship Rights of the Chakmas of Arunachal Pradesh.

I am asking the Home Minister to look into the matter.

With regards.

Yours sincerely,
[P.V. Narasimha Rao]

Shri Somnath Chatterjee, MP
21, Ashoka Road
New Delhi

Copy to : Shri [illegible] Chakma, Convenor, Committee for Citizenship [illegible] Chakmas of Arunachal Pradesh, [illegible] Vihar, Old Tower [illegible], New Delhi-110 002.

for ([illegible])

APPENDIX X

SOMNATH CHATTERJEE
MEMBER OF PARLIAMENT
Leader, CPI(M), Lok Sabha

[illegible]
P-514, Raja Basanta Roy Road,
Calcutta-700 029
[illegible]
21, Ashoka Road,
New Delhi-110 001

New Delhi
March 31, 1992

Dear Prime Minister

Enclosed please find an Appeal from the Committee for Citizenship Rights of the Chakmas of Arunachal Pradesh in which they have mentioned the serious difficulties they are facing in the matter of employment, educational facilities, etc.

It is stated that about 30,000 Chakma and Hajong tribals had migrated to India in 1964 from former East Pakistan and were rehabilitated by the Government of India in Arunachal Pradesh. They are not being given employment in Arunachal Pradesh nor are trade licences, ration cards being issued to them. They are also denied all educational facilities.

It is a matter of concern that the people who are rehabilitated by the Government of India in a part of the country are not being given minimum facilities which citizens of the country are entitled to enjoy.

May I earnestly request you to please consider the Appeal sympathetically so that facilities are given to the people who have already been settled, as stated in the Appeal.

With kind regards,

Yours sincerely,

(Somnath Chatterjee)

Encls: As above

Shri P.V. Narasimha Rao,
Prime Minister,
New Delhi.

Copy to: Shri Subimal Bikash Chakma, President,
Committee for Citizenship Rights of the
Chakmas of Arunachal Pradesh,
Ashok Buddha Vihar,
Old Power House Road, Rajghat,
New Delhi-110002

(Somnath Chatterjee)

APPENDIX XI

MANORANJAN BHAKTA, M.P.
Chairman
Estimates Committee, Lok Sabha
No. 18(CHEC)/92

Office : 52-B, Parliament House,
New Delhi-110001
Phone : 3017464 & 3034791

23rd March, 1992

Dear Shri

I am enclosing an appeal from the President Committee for Citizenship Rights of the Chakmas of Arunchal Pradesh requesting for grant of Indian Citizenship to the Chakmas who migrated to India from East Pakistan (now Bangladesh) and settled in Arunchal Pradesh by the Government of India.

It is alleged that Chakmas have been subjected to all sorts of harrassment and the State Government has also deprived them of the educational, employment and trading facilities. The appeal is self-explanatory. Similar appeal was also forwarded by me on 26th November, 91.

Please examine the matter and take appropriate action.

With regards,

Yours sincerely,

(MANORANJAN BHAKTA)

Shri S.B.Chavan,
Minister of Home Affairs,
India,
New Delhi.

Copy to:

Shri Subimal Bikash Chakma,
Committee for Citizenship Rights
of the Chakmas of Arunchal Pradesh
Ashok Buddha Vihar, Old Power House Road,
Rajghat, New Delhi - 110 002.

(MANORANJAN BHAKTA)

APPENDIX XII

GOVERNMENT OF ARUNACHAL PRADESH
OFFICE OF THE CIRCLE OFFICER : DIYUN CIRCLE : DISTRICT CHANGLANG :
ARUNACHAL PRADESH

NO. FPSO-3/90-91/ Dated Diyun, the 31st Oct'91.

CIRCULAR

With reference to the sig. of D.C. Changlang vide msg No. CS/PP-[illegible]/89/99 of 25/10/91 it is to inform all concerned that issue of Ration Cards to refugees like Chakma, Hajong and Tibetans has been banned by the Government.

Hence no Ration Cards will be issued/renewed for Chakmas and Hajongs with effect from 1st November'91 onward.

Sd/- T. YUSLI, UDC
for Circle Officer,
DIYUN

Memo NO. FPSO-3/90-91/ Dated Diyun, the 31st Oct'91.
Copy to :- All [illegible] concerned GBs for information. They are directed to surrender their ration cards to this Office accordingly.

2. The Manager, Diyun Coop. General Stores, Diyun for information. No FPS items should be issued to refugees from 1st Nov'91 onward.

3. The FPS P.L. Singpho, [illegible] for information and strict compliance. He is also directed to act as above.

4. The M/S [illegible], FPS Innao for strict compliance as above.

5. The Deputy Commissioner, Changlang District, Changlang for information please.

6. Office notice board.

7. Office copy.

(T. YUSLI) UDC
Circle Officer,
DIYUN

APPENDIX XIII

GOVERNMENT OF ARUNACHAL PRADESH – ITANAGAR

No.Pol-21/81 Dated the Itanagar 29th Sept/80

To

The Deputy Commissioner
Khonsa, Tirap Dist. (A.P.)

Sir,

I am directed to refer to your letter No. CA-103/78/75 dated 20/6/80 regarding employment facilities to Chakmas/Hajongs/and other refugees under the government. The matter is under examination and therefore no appointment be given to Chakmas/Hajongs/Yobins and Tibetan refugees till a final decision is arrived at. Those who are already in govt. services may continue, but should not be permanent.

Further instruction in the matter will follow.

Sd/-

(B. Hussain)
Secretary (Political)
Itanagar

No.Pol-21/80 Dated Itanagar the 29th Sept/80

Copy to :-

The all Deputy Commissioners/Adl. Deputy Commissioners in Arunachal Pradesh.

Sd/-

(B. Hussain)
Secretary (Political)
Itanagar

APPENDIX XIV

Kabindra Purkayastha
Member of Parliament
(Lok Sabha)

147, South Avenue,
New Delhi-110011
Phone [illegible]

[illegible],
Silchar-[illegible]
Phone [illegible]

31.7.95.

Dear Shri Chavanjee,

Please find herewith a copy of memorandum addressed to you by the President,Committee for Citizenship Rights of the Chakmas of Arunachal Pradesh'praying for immediate awarding of citizenship right to the Chakmas and Hajongs to enable them to exercise their fundamental right to frachise in the 1996 Parliamentary Election.

It is a longstanding genuine demand of the Chakmas. In spite of assurances given on the floor of the Parliament, the Govt. have not yet implemented it for which the Chakmas and Hajongs have been facing serious problems and trouble. Only because of this,they are still deprived of their legi-timate rights.

As the matter of awarding citizenship right is a matter within the jurisdiction of the Central Govt. and the Govt. already declared to award citizenship to the Chakmas and Hajongs,I believe that nothing can be stood on the way.

So,I request you immediate notification and implement the assurance given time ti time by the Govt.

With kind regards,

Yours sincerly,

[signature] [illegible]

Shri S.B.Chavan,
Minister of Home Affairs,
North Block,New Delhi.

APPENDIX XV

ELECTION COMMISSION OF INDIA

Nirvachan Sadan, Ashoka Road, New Delhi-110001

No.23/ARUN/2007 Dated 1st February, 2007

To

The Chief Electoral Officer,
Arunachal Pradesh, Itanagar

Subject:- Special summary revision of electoral rolls of 4 constituencies in Arunachal Pradesh w.r.t. 1.1.2007 as qualifying date- schedule /guidelines - regarding

Sir,

I am directed to state that the Commission has decided to conduct a special summary revision of the electoral rolls of 34-Doimukh (ST), 46-Chowkham (ST), 49-Bordumsa Diyun and 50-Miao (ST) Assembly Constituencies in the State of Arunachal Pradesh w.r.t. 1.1.2007 as qualifying date. The Commission has issued special guidelines for the said revision which is enclosed at Annexure I. The schedule for the revision is enclosed at Annexure -II. The Commission has directed that the guidelines shall be scrupulously followed in the current revision process. Please inform all concerned immediately and take action accordingly.

2. As mentioned under para 2(1) of the guidelines, you are requested to immediately forward proposals for appointment of EROs and the Appellate Authority for these Constituencies in consultation with the State Govt.

Yours faithfully,

(K. AJAYA KUMAR)
SECRETARY

APPENDIX XVI

AN APPEAL

As you are aware, the refugee problem is a burning issue in our peaceful State of Arunachal Pradesh, since long back. In order to preserve the peaceful atmosphere of our tribal State, we have been raising repeated demands for deportation of such refugees, particularly Chakma and Hajong refugees, from our State which is yet to be acceded to by the Central Government.

This refugee problem has reached such a grave situation that it is creating serious law and order problems, threatening the demographic aspect, peaceful co-existence and the very identity of the indigenous people of the State. The unlawful activities of such refugees has put the bonafide people of the State into much embarrassment. Their illegal settlement in the State, demand for permanent citizenship rights and misrepresentation of facts and figures in various forums are creating panic among the bonafide people and tarnishing the image of our State. Their demand for permanent settlement in the whole districts of Tirap, Changlang, Lohit, Lower Subansiri and Papum Pare and preparation of map to strengthen their false claims are provocating the bonafide people of our State. They dishonoured the verdict of the Hon'ble Supreme Court which is highly objectionable. Who is responsible for non-implementation of the Supreme Court verdict?

Considering the serious nature and complexity of the problem, an All Party Legislature meeting was held on 6th September 1995 under the Chairmanship of Hon'ble Chief Minister Shri Gegong Apang, wherein, it was decided to organise a Peoples' Referendum Rally in the Raj Gandhi Stadium at Naharlagun on 20th September 1995, demanding immediate deportation of Chakma and Hajong refugees from the State in which, people from all walks of life, irrespective of party affiliations, caste and creed, will participate.

We highly appreciate this important and genuine decision in the better interest of our indigenous people of the State. We appeal to all of you, irrespective of party affiliations, caste and creed, to ensure your participation in the rally and express your resentment and rejection of the presence of Chakma and Hajong refugees in the State and thus to make the rally a grand success.

"WE DEMAND CHAKMA AND HAJONG REFUGEES TO QUIT ARUNACHAL"

JAI HIND

Published by : Organising Committee Peoples' Referendum Rally.

APPENDIX XVII

OFFICE OF THE
ALL ARUNACHAL PRADESH STUDENTS' UNION

Memo No.AAPSU/GS-1B/04-86/01 Dated Itanagar the 1st Aug 1986.

To

The Hon'ble Chief Minister,
Arunachal Pradesh,
ITANAGAR-791 111.

Sir,

The All Arunachal Pradesh Students' Union (AAPSU) in its general meeting held at Pasighat (Arunachal Pradesh) on 15th, 16th and 17th July 1986 resolved after detailed deliberation to place the following Ultimatum to the Govt. of Arunachal Pradesh. The meeting also resolved to urge upon the Government of Arunachal Pradesh to concede the demands mentioned in the charter within the month of September, 1986 failing which the AAPSU will be left with no other alternative but to take agitational path.

THE CHARTER OF DEMANDS:

1. REFUGEE PROBLEM:

Whereas, Arunachal Pradesh is the most sensitive border state of the Republic of India where it was necessary to restrict entry of even genuine Indian citizens without valid Inner Line Permits;

Whereas, there are already about 80,000 (Eighty thousand) refugees in a total population of approximately seven lakh people in Arunachal Pradesh;

Whereas, in many areas like Miao Circle in Tirap District where out of a total population of about 57,000 people only 12,000 are native population, the refugees have outnumbered the local population and thereby changed the whole demographic pattern;

Whereas, the Arunachal Assembly has been adopting many resolutions from time to time (28-3-77, 17-8-77, 28-12-82 and 23-11-82 etc.) for deportation of refugees but have failed to do so;

Whereas, other neighbouring states have taken concrete steps and have consistently been deporting foreigners;

Whereas, the Bengal Eastern Frontier Regulation Act, 1873 and Chinhill Act ensure the protection of the interest of the native tribal population whose identity is at stake today;

Contd...2/-

APPENDIX XVIII

CONFIDENTIAL

GOVERNMENT OF INDIA
ARUNACHAL PRADESH ADMINISTRATION
SHILLONG.

No.RRS-1[illegible]/[illegible]/Part II   Dated Shillong, the [illegible] May, 1973.

To

1. The Deputy Commissioner, Khonsa.
2. The Extra Assistant Commissioner, Miao.
3. The Deputy Commissioner Lohit Dist. Tezu.
4. The Deputy Commissioner Subansiri, Ziro.

Sub :- CHAKMA REFUGEES IN ARUNACHAL PRADESH.

Sir,

I am directed to say that the following informations are urgently required by the Ministry of Home Affairs. Information in respect of Sl.1-7 have been furnished locally but Sl.No.8 and 9 could not be ~~[illegible]~~ complite with as the same is not available in this Deptt.

2. The information in respect of Sl.8 and 9 in so far they are concerned with your District may kindly be furnished urgently for onward transmission to Ministry.

1) Number of Chakma Refugees in Arunachal Pradesh.
2) Name of villages where they have been settled.
3) Quantum of land alloted to each family.
4) Irrigation facilities.
5) Communication.
6) Marketing facilities for agricultural products.
7) Whether some of the Chakmas unauthorisedly settled in Deep area in Bordumsa of Tirap District.
8) Whether there is any scope to improve the cultivable land alloted to them.
9) Whether the refugees have obtained some land belonging to the local Singphos of Tirap District by payment of cash.

Yours faithfully,

(C.M. Smith)
Under Secretary & Ex-Officio Director of Rehabilitation and Settlement,
Arunachal Pradesh Admn., Shillong.

*****

APPENDIX XIX

GOVT. OF ARUNACHAL PRADESH
OFFICE OF THE CIRCLE OFFICER : DIYUN : CHANGLANG DISTRICT.

No. DYN/REV/TL-[illegible]
Dated Diyun the [illegible] May [illegible]

PROVISIONAL TRADE LICENSE.

Shri/Smti [illegible]
son/daughter/wife of ____________________
an inhabitant/settler of [illegible] village is permitted to run a shop at [illegible] to sell the following items subject to the conditions prescribed below he/she has accepted.

Type of shop to be run :- [illegible] Annual fee to be paid by the licence holder.
[illegible]

C O N D I T I O N S :-

1. The trade licence holder is to pay annual fee in advance against each category of items mentioned above for which he/she is authorised to deal with the licence holder [illegible] his/her business. But if he/she intends to engage more than two persons he/she will have to pay fee [illegible] for third and fifth additional hand respectively; and in no case any permit holder be allowed to engaged more than five persons in his/her shop.

2. The shop and its surroundings will have to kept clean all times.

3. No credit sale will be allowed to the local tribals and others; loan and advance are also not given to any one.

4. No exciseable articles and liquor of any kind be sold in the shop.

5. No gambling be allowed.

6. He/She is to sell all the articles at the rate fixed by the rate board from time to time.

7. He/She will not sell any items except those category of articles mentioned in his/her licence.

8. He/She will not sublet his/her shop to any other persons.

9. This permit shall remain valid for a calendar year and renewable on expiry, subject to satisfactory performance in the past period.

Contd. P/-2.

APPENDIX XX

COMMITTEE FOR CITIZENSHIP RIGHTS OF THE CHAKMAS OF ARUNACHAL PRADESH

Office : Ashok Buddha Vihar, Old Power House Road, Rajghat, New Delhi – 110 002
Telephone : 3312927, 3253483

[illegible]

AN APPEAL

This historic 3-day Hunger strike is being organised by the Committee for Citizenship Rights of the Chakmas of Arunachal Pradesh as a mark of protest against the Govt. of India's [illegible] approach and the state Govt's opposition to the implementation of the policy decision taken by the Union Govt. to grant Citizenship Rights to the 65,000 Chakma and Hajong migrants of Arunachal Pradesh. Actually these Buddhist Chakmas and Hindu Hajongs who hail from Chittagong Hill Tracts and Mymensingh district respectively of the erstwhile East Pakistan legally migrated to India and were rehabilitated in North East Frontier Agency (NEFA) province under the auspices of the Ministry of rehabilitation, Govt. of India way back in 1964. About 4.5 lakhs refugees from East Pakistan were Rehabilitated in West Bengal, Assam, Tripura, Bihar, Andaman and Nicobar Island in this period. While all their counter-parts settled elsewhere are recognised as full-fledged Indian Citizens, it is unfortunate that the Chakmas and Hajongs settled and rehabilitated in Arunachal Pradesh (NEFA became Union Territory of Arunachal Pradesh in 1972) are yet to be conferred this right.

Even the Assam Accord of 1985 failed to provide them citizenship rights. While granting citizenship rights to all person of Indian origin who have come over to Assam on or before 25th March, 1971, the Assam Accord does not say anything about the Chakmas and Hajongs who came over to Assam in 1964 but happen to be in Arunachal Pradesh at the time of commencement of the Assam Accord by mere accident of history. It may be noted that the Indira-Mujib pact of 1972 which formed the basis of Assam Accord also makes it mandatory on the Govt. of India to recognise all refugees from erstwhile East Pakistan who came over to India before March 25th, 1971 as citizens of India.

A letter from former Minister of State for Home, Shri M.M. Jacob to Shri Laeta Umbrey, ex M.P. from Arunachal Pradesh dated 23rd September, 1992 has revealed that a central team had visited Arunachal Pradesh to study the problem of the Chakmas in 1982. The team recommended for the grant of citizenship rights but it was never implemented. Describing the Chakmas as refugees settled in Arunachal Pradesh "under a definite plan of rehabilitation" Mr. Jacob further stated that **"Being refugees from Bangladesh (read East Pakistan) who came over to India between 1964 and 71, they are eligible to the grant of Citizenship according to the policy of the Govt. on the subject and most of these refugees have already been granted citizenship".**

If that is so, why is the Union Govt. silent when all the constitutional rights of the Chakmas and Hajongs are being taken away ? The State Govt. had banned employment rights to the Chakmas and Hajongs through an official Circular No. Pol – 21/80 dated 29-9-1980; Issue of Ration Cards to Chakmas had been banned on 31.10.91 and the right of the Chakmas to have items of Public Distribution System (PDS) has been banned in Feb 1994. It is pertinent to mention here that it was

APPENDIX XXI

Peoples' Rights Organisation

(PRO)

Presents a Report on

The Question of Indian Citizenship Rights of the Stateless Chakmas and Hajongs of Arunachal Pradesh

Index

❑❑❑